WHERE TO GO IN ROMANIA

HAROLD DENNIS-JONES

SETTLE PRESS
HIPPOCRENE BOOKS INC.

STOP PRESS See p126

Subsidised travel between "socialist" countries was cancelled in 1991. Budapest–Bucharest on international trains now costs £96 2nd class return. You're charged express and seat reservation supplements plus *three times* normal fares. In Hungary you pay in hard currency with the Romanian fare calculated at roughly 1 ft = 1 leu.

In Romania all bills are now paid in lei. Using hard currency, the "free" exchange rate of roughly four times the "official" rate (£1 = 400 lei instead of 100), reduces Romanian–Hungarian travel costs greatly.

To save money you can take ordinary trains to a main town near the frontier, rebook on an international train to the first main stop beyond the border (*not* the border station itself: that's not allowed), then catch a third train.

Alternatively, check for border-crossing buses between, say, Szeged and Arad and Debrecan and Oradea. Romanian hotels change money speedily.

Texts, maps and photographs © 1991 Harold Dennis-Jones
Maps designed and executed by Harold Dennis-Jones
All rights reserved. No part of this publication
may be reproduced or transmitted in any form or
by any means without permission.
First published by Settle Press
10 Boyne Terrace Mews
London W11 3LR
Revised edition 1992

Cover photograph of the Clock Tower, Sighisoara (Chapter Nine) by Harold Dennis-Jones. The historical Dracula was born barely 100m from the spot from which this photograph was taken.

ISBN (Paperback) 1 872876 01 3

Published in USA by
Hippocrene Books Inc
171 Madison Avenue, New York

Printed by Villiers Publications Ltd
26a Shepherds Hill, London N6 5AH

Contents

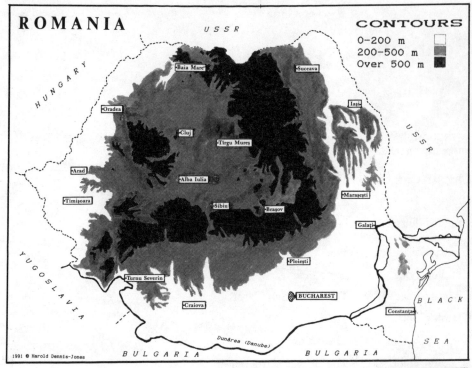

ROMANIA

CONTOURS

0-200 m
200-500 m
Over 500 m

USSR

HUNGARY

·Baia Mare·
·Suceava·

·Oradea·
Iași

·Cluj·
USSR

·Tîrgu Mureș·

·Arad·
·Alba Iulia·

·Timișoara·
·Sibiu·
·Brașov·
·Mărășești·

·Galați·

·Ploiești·

YUGOSLAVIA

·Turnu Severin·
BLACK

🏛 BUCHAREST
Constanța·

·Craiova·

SEA

Dunărea (Danube)

BULGARIA
BULGARIA

1991 © Harold Dennis-Jones

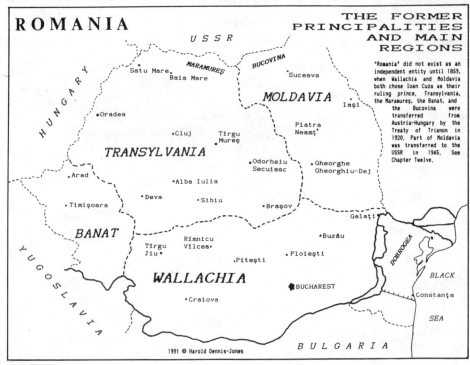

ROMANIA

THE FORMER PRINCIPALITIES AND MAIN REGIONS

USSR

MARAMUREȘ
BUCOVINA

Satu Mare·
·Suceava·
Baia Mare

MOLDAVIA

HUNGARY
·Oradea·
Iași

·Cluj·
Tîrgu Mureș·
Piatra Neamț·

TRANSYLVANIA

·Odorheiu Secuiesc·
·Gheorghe Gheorghiu-Dej·

·Arad·
·Alba Iulia·

·Deva·
·Sibiu·
·Brașov·

·Timișoara·
Galați·

BANAT
·Buzău·

Rîmnicu Vîlcea·
Tîrgu Jiu·
·Ploiești·

DOBROGEA

·Pitești·

WALLACHIA
BLACK

🏛 BUCHAREST
Constanța·

·Craiova·

SEA

YUGOSLAVIA

"Romania" did not exist as an independent entity until 1859, when Wallachia and Moldavia both chose Ioan Cuza as their ruling prince. Transylvania, the Maramureș, the Banat, and the Bucovina were transferred from Austria-Hungary by the Treaty of Trianon in 1920. Part of Moldavia was transferred to the USSR in 1945. See Chapter Twelve.

BULGARIA

1991 © Harold Dennis-Jones

1. The Call of Romania

Everyone knows that in the early months of 1990 Romanians were having a difficult time. Revolution had freed them suddenly from forty years of increasingly vicious repression, and the future wasn't at all clear. In the English-speaking world everyone also knows the reputation – wholly undeserved – inflicted on Transylvania by Bram Stoker's novel *Dracula*.

Unfortunately, that's the limit of almost everyone's knowledge. Even the august Royal Geographical Society's Expedition Advisory Centre announced in April 1990 that Romania was a "new destination", just "opening up". When challenged, they justified the statement with the assertion that people were only now beginning to go there.

The facts are different. Romania has been actively encouraging visitors for over 25 years, and has developed a sizable, though till now badly managed and poorly publicised, tourist industry. So far from just beginning to be noticeable, holiday bookings in April 1990 were appreciably down. Throughout this period you've never needed an "expedition" to explore Romania. The only restriction, from about 1970, was that you couldn't stay in private houses and, more recently, that you had to exchange a modest $10 (£6.25) a day during your visit. In January 1990 the Provisional Government's rescinded these two laws as one of their first acts.

Since 1967 I've been travelling the length and breadth of the country on foot, by ordinary car, by train, by bus, and by plane. And what a country I've discovered! It's not just the beauty of its landscapes and its ancient cities, and the efficient design and operation of its modern Black Sea coast resorts, that are impressive. The people's character, their well-preserved and highly individual culture, and the unquenchable hospitality you meet – especially in mountain areas – make touring there immensely attractive. But no one has bothered to make this clear to potential visitors. Romania till now has been ridiculously neglected, even by those who pretend to knowledge and should know better.

The country's physical make-up is unusual. Roughly one-third is flood-plain created by the Danube and its vast number of tributaries. One third is rolling plateau at an average altitude around 500 m. The rest consists of mountains rising to 2543 m.

The mountains are mostly part of the huge Carpathian range. Inside Romania they form a vast horseshoe whose westward-facing opening is partly blocked by the separate clump of the lower Bihor mountains, with peaks up to 1834 m.

We tend to think that mountains must all be gaunt, forbidding, threatening. The Carpathians certainly have their share of impressive gorges and rock faces, and good skiing areas. But many slopes are covered with miles and miles of varied forests. "As far as

5

the eye can reach is a sea of green treetops" is how Bram Stoker's Jonathan Harker describes the view from the Count's castle in *Dracula*. It's absolutely accurate. Stoker never went nearer Romania than the British Museum's Reading Room. To manufacture his superb story he distorted all the facts surrounding the historical "Draculea". But it's clear that the books the BM provided in the 1890s described the country far more accurately than anything you'll find in bookshops or your local library today.

What's specially striking about the Carparthian forests is the feeling of friendliness they give off. Nowhere do you feel as threatened as you do in, say, Germany's forests. Interestingly enough, Romania's folk tales reflect this kindliness. Their tone is totally different from the continuous terrors of the Grimm brothers' German stories. And where the forests cease, long, lofty green slopes often continue to make you welcome. Munte Gaina's flat mountaintop, scene of the centuries-old Maidens' Fair every third Sunday in July on one of the Bihor's higher points, 1486 m above the sea, is a decidedly happy, appealing spot.

Rolling upland plateau land fringes the Carpathians' outer curves, fills the horseshoe's inner ring, and occupies both the Bucovina in Moldavia's far north and much of the Dobrogea's rectangle between Danube and Black Sea coast. It has a different kind of appeal. Its slopes are covered by smaller, broken stretches of woodland, by orchards, and vineyards. Gentle streams sparkle in its valleys, as well as large rivers like the Somes, the Mures, the Cris in all its branches, and all their tributaries.

Much of this hilly land is extremely fertile, and the villages, built in different styles in different parts of the

country – you can see typical houses collected together and re-erected in Bucharest's excellent Village Museum – display both the country people's individuality and a tremendous degree of traditional craftsmanship. Many have changed very little in the last centuries.

The plains have less appeal. One flat area however, the Danube's extraordinary Delta, is unique. Of its 434,000 ha barely one-seventh is land, and four-fifths of that is liable to flooding. The watery area is filled mostly with floating reed beds that permit only constantly changing channels apart from three main shipping routes leading to inland ports.

The Delta's wildlife ranges from what look like equatorial forests to insect-eating plants, animals galore, a huge variety of fish (including the sturgeon that gives us caviar), and a host of birds, including Europe's only pelican-breeding colonies. Yet this isn't Romania's only region of outstanding wildlife interest. Brown bear, Carpathian stag, chamois, lynx and endless other creatures inhabit the Carparthians. In hard winters wolves move south from the USSR seeking food. Numerous laws and Nature Reserves protect animals, birds, plants, and natural land formations.

There are skiing areas in the Southern Carpathians, reasonably well equipped with modern tows and lifts. Modern coast resorts such as Mamaia, excellently laid out on a narrow sandbar separating the sea from a freshwater lagoon, and a string of smaller spots closer to the Bulgarian border, provide everything the beach holiday addict can wish for – including excursions to the Danube delta, sightseeing among very striking Greek and Roman remains, visits to magnificent monastery churches in the

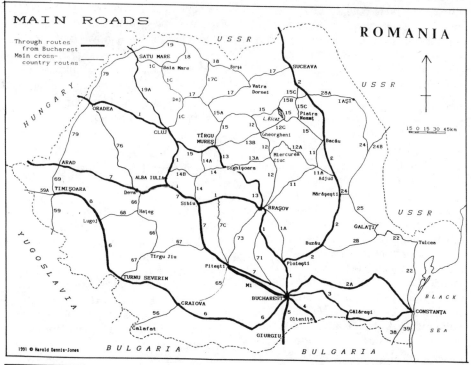

MAIN ROADS

ROMANIA

Through routes from Bucharest
Main cross-country routes

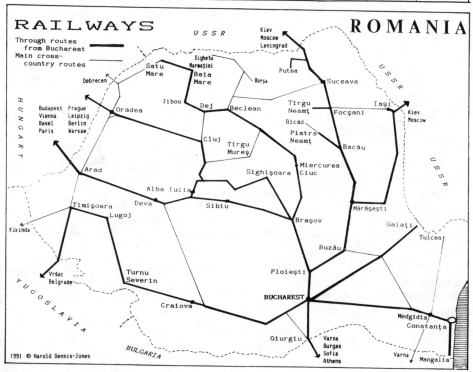

RAILWAYS

ROMANIA

Through routes from Bucharest
Main cross-country routes

Bucovina whose outside as well as inside walls are covered with magnificent 16th century frescos, and to places even further afield. The churches have been for years on UNESCO's "World Heritage" list.

For anyone enterprising enough to tour Romania by car or public transport there's a mass of lovely towns as well as superb scenery – places like Cluj, Iasi, Sibiu, Timisoara, Brasov, Sighisoara, Oradea, Arad, Alba Iulia, Suceava, and many others. There are magnificent Orthodox monasteries throughout the country, mostly tucked away in hidden spots. Many were built to serve also as fortress–refuges against invaders. Several have preserved their fortifying walls. Moldovita, Sucevita, and Dragomirna in northern Moldavia are outstanding. In the Salaj, in the remote northwestern Maramures, and throughout the country you'll find more than seven hundred amazing small village wooden churches, often with amazingly tall, slim spires. The highest soars over 60 m from the ground. They range in date from the 14th to 19th centuries. Some still retain traces of original wall-paintings. All were built without the use of a single nail. They are mind-boggling examples of skilled joinery.

What's more, you'll meet a range of varied cultures and traditions inside modern Romania's boundaries. There are some 2 million Hungarians and Szeklers in the country, and sizable numbers of ethnic Germans, as well as smaller pockets of Serbs, Slovaks, Russians, Tatars, Turks, and a few remaining Jews. Gipsies exist everywhere. Some long ago became known as outstanding musicians and craftsmen, while the Transylvanian Germans were famous for church organs and lovely handwoven carpets.

But every nationality provides its own skills. Till recently their settlements tended to be quite separate. In one village, you'd speak German, in the next Hungarian, and so on. Things are different now.

If you add to all this a mass of fascinating and often unusual museums, such as Sibiu's Village Technology collection and little Sibiel's breathtaking display of icons painted on glass, still-flourishing age-old handicrafts, folk music that reaches directly back to 16th-century traditions, and costumes the same as modern Romania's Dacian ancestors were wearing in the 2nd century AD, and set this against a network of modern roads, reasonably adequate public transport, hotels, campsites, and private accommodation you'll have some idea of the delights that Romania can provide.

The old principalities explained in Chapter Twelve, form the basis of my description of Romania, not because of nostalgia but because they correspond to natural geographic regions.

In touring through the country I've indicated where campsites are available, but cannot guarantee that changes may not occur. Hotels and travel routes are less subject to change. I notice only a few of Romania's many Nature Reserves, and only the most popular mountain walking areas. Additional information is available from the Romanian National Tourist Offices.

2. The Best of Romania

In a country as rich and varied as Romania "the best" becomes a matter of opinion. Here are my own choices.

Coast resorts   MAMAIA, with its magnificent 10 km-long sandy beach, its excellent trees, shrubs, flowers, and well-planned layout, is outstanding. If you prefer smaller spots, try EFORIE NORD, NEPTUN, or CAP AURORA.

Ski resorts   POIANA BRASOV in the Southern Carpathians's Transylvanian side, SINAIA on the Wallachian, and PREDEAL astride the pass between, are three sound skiing bases with modern facilities.

Cities   In Transylvania the older central areas of CLUJ (or CLUJ-NAPOCA as it's officially called), TIRGU MURES, SIBIU, BRASOV, ORADEA, ARAD, ALBA IULIA, AND SATU MARE are well worth seeing. SIGHISOARA's citadel area and the baroque square below are magnificent, though the new town around them is messy. The Banat's capital, TIMISOARA, is impressive, as are the old parts of SUCEAVA and IASI in Moldavia. TIRGU JIU in western Wallachia is worth visiting just to see the sculpture ensemble that Brancusi planned but was prevented from completing. CONSTANTA in the Dobrogea is worth a visit for its beautifully preserved and well displayed Roman remains.

Scenic regions   Almost anywhere except the plains. The following regions are outstanding: the BIHOR moutain mass east of Oradea; the FAGARAS range on the Transylvanian side of the Southern Carpathians; most of the Eastern (Moldavian) Carpathians, including especially the Ceahlau massif, Lake Bicaz, and the passes into Transylvania; the ARGES region on the Carpathians' southern side; the RETEZAT and other lonely mountain areas near it; the Danube's once-turbulent IRON GATES GORGE to their southwest; the "PAINTED CHURCHES" circuit in Moldavia; in quieter vein, the whole of the MARAMURES; and the SALAJ region between Cluj and Satu Mare in Western Transylvania.

Walking holidays   Scenic regions mentioned above provide excellent walking. Most have extensive ranges of marked paths. For an easy, car-free introduction to the Carpathians however you may find it simpler to book summer accommodation (or buy a straightforward package tour) in one of the three accepted winter ski resorts. All offer excellent summer walking on clearly marked paths, with people available in the resorts to give you the extra information about path difficulty, timing, etc that walkers usually need. Language is also less problem here. For your next visit you can extend your range.

Gentler walking (though distances can be long) is provided by the DANUBE DELTA's restricted areas of terra firma. The most interesting paths link

Crisan to the Caraorman Forest and beyond; and Sulina at the Delta's main mouth to Letea, its forest, and on to Periprava on the Chilia Arm that . forms the boundary between Romania and the USSR.

Birdwatching and wildlife The most obvious choice for birdwatchers is the DANUBE DELTA, though you have to make your own arrangements. The pelicans' arrival in April–May is exciting, and there's a vast variety of other birdlife. Wildlife in the Delta holds many delights, as it does in the RETEZAT NATIONAL PARK. The country has scores of Nature Reserves which are mostly in good condition despite occasional foci of appalling pollution. There is little sign as yet of acid rain.

Museums Museums are usually the last things I explore. They can't be ignored, but you need to know the country before you can appreciate them. In Romania however some are so outstanding that they deserve a special "not to be missed even first time round" mention. Bucharest's VILLAGE MUSEUM has a world-famous collection of regional houses and handicrafts – outstanding for the specialist, too vast for most ordinary people to absorb even in several visits, but nevertheless a "must" for any visitor to Bucharest.

The little-publicised open-air section of Cluj's ETHNOGRAPHIC MUSEUM, located on an open hillside above the town, is much more manageable and thoroughly enjoyable. The MUSEUM OF VILLAGE TECHNOLOGY at Dumbrava Sibiului near Sibiu, with its stunning collection of handmade agricultural implements, waterwheels, handmills, mining equipment, handlooms, and the like is

pure delight. The virtually unknown ICONS ON GLASS COLLECTION in the tiny village of Sibiel literally took my breath away the first time I saw it.

Sibiu's BRUKENTHAL MUSEUM is charming, an aristocrat's collection from the days of Transylvania's great prosperity. The national FOLK ART MUSEUM is magnificent and housed in a superb 1835 building at 107 Calea Victoriei in Bucharest, but like the Village Museum a little overpowering.

Archaeological sites Not what you immediately associate with Romania. Some however are well worth special visits.

These include the MOSAIC PAVEMENT and other remains in Constanta's port area; the TROPAEUM TRAJANI erected at Adamclisi by the Roman Emperor Trajan in AD 109 to celebrate his conquest of Dacia (roughly modern Romania): and the remains of the ancient Greek city of HISTRIA (17th century BC on) between Constanta and Tulcea.

You can hunt out some extraordinary EARLY CHRISTIAN CHURCHES – two built underground in the Dobrogea, and an astonishing structure of disputed date at Densus, south of Hunedoara. It's seemingly based on a Roman provincial commander's mausoleum. The Dacians' ancient stronghold of SARMIZEGETUSA in the Orastie Mountains is worth exploring, as is the Roman town of the same name on flat ground to its west. Many towns, including Suceava, still have the ruins of impressive MEDIEVAL CITADELS, and in Transylvania scores of VILLAGE CITADELS are fascinating.

3. Planning Your Holiday

What do you expect from a trip to Romania? Seaside relaxation in blazing summer sun? Good skiing and cheerful winter evening entertainment? A chance to explore, maybe not too strenuously, an unknown country? Or something physically and mentally more active – birdwatching, perhaps, or walking in the mountains, or discovering new forms of architecture, new handicrafts, new music, new cooking, an entire new culture? Romania offers all this and more.

Package Tour . . . ?

The package tours on offer are stereotyped but usually efficiently organised and inexpensive. You can have your summer week or fortnight on the Black Sea coast or in a modern mountain resort such as Poiana Brasov. In summer you can also take coach tours that often include other countries. In winter you can ski at three modern or modernised resorts in the Southern Carpathians, Romania's highest part. These are all good holidays, and not ruinously pricey.

They don't in themselves however show you much of Romania. Modern coast resorts, however relaxing and however well-planned, are much the same the world over, apart from variations in scenery and sometimes in the food and drinks they provide. The same applies to ski spots. If you want an effort-free holiday that shows you at least a little of what's unique in Romania you can opt for a fortnight's summer package tour either on the coast or in the mountains and take as many available excursions as possible.

From either area day trips to Bucharest are possible. From the coast you can visit also the Danube Delta (though in a very limited way), nearby vineyards, various archaeological sites, resorts in Bulgaria and, on longer trips, the magnificent "Painted Churches" of the Bucovina. You'll also be able to travel by air to places further afield, such as Kiev or Istanbul.

From Poiana Brasov in the mountains you can visit fine towns such as Brasov, Sibiu, and Sighisoara. You can see parts of the remarkable chains of "village citadels" built by Germans specially brought from Saxony to guard the Magyar kingdom's frontiers in medieval days. With luck you'll be able to visit at least some of the lovely Arges region and some of its outstanding historical sites. A very long day out may even take you to Northern Moldavia's unique churches.

If you choose a summer package in a mountain resort you'll also find it possible to spend your days walking.

. . . or on your own?

You can have a more adventurous time, and see a lot more of Romania and the Romanians, by travelling independently – though this, as everywhere, brings its own problems.

If you take your own car you'll find little difficulty getting around inside Romania apart from hotels being full in high summer and petrol occasionally running short (fill up every time you pass a filling station – and carry a spare can). On the other hand, it's a long way to drive getting there – unless of course, you've plenty of time, more than one driver, and things to see or do along your route. Channel port–German Autobahn–Vienna–Budapest–Oradea is the easiest approach.

As an alternative to driving the whole way, consider a fly–drive package. Some of these include hotel bookings and maybe petrol coupons. They make touring easy, but compel you to follow a fixed route.

If you want to be totally free you must either use campsites, or take a chance on hotels being fully booked, or on having to find private-house accommodation when you possibly don't feel like making the effort. You'd best also keep picnic food and drink (bottles of mineral water or soft drinks) in the car in case you don't come on suitable restaurants. The towns are OK, but you may not find many places to eat or drink in outside them.

Almost complete independence is attained by using a motor caravan or towing a trailer. I say "almost complete" because it's advisable to use only organised campsites where your static gear will be watched while you're away or else to arrange with a private family to use a corner of their land and rely on their eyes while you're out for the day (see Chapter Thirteen).

Touring by public transport – plane, rail, and bus – is also possible. It's an ideal way of making contact with local people of every sort. The mechanics of getting timetable information, buying tickets, etc can however be somewhat different from most Western countries, and you need to get them clear in your mind in advance. You'll find details in Chapter Thirteen. You'll also find suggestions there about how best to book accommodation, which may be a problem in high summer unless you've planned your route and booked well in advance.

If you've plenty of time, and don't expect Western luxuries all the way, public transport touring, choosing your next destination on the spur of the moment, can be a wonderful way of getting to know this unexpected country. You should however arm yourself in advance with all the information you can. It's not always easy to find it on the spot.

InterRail passes are valid for the under-26s in Romania. Senior citizens' Rail Europe cards give you no reductions. Fares however are very low by Western standards.

When to go

Summers can be very hot and winters very cold – including on the Black Sea coast, which closes down in mid-September and begins to operate again only in May at the earliest. The climate however is surprisingly variable, with mild winters not uncommon, and rain possible in summer despite the heat.

For fuller details see Chapter Thirteen.

4. Bucharest

We spell it Bucharest. The Germans and Hungarians write it Bukarest. The French use the form Bucarest. To the Romanians themselves the city is Bucuresti. Why all outsiders should have altered the sound of the second u, and why Westerners should have abandoned the sh sound of what Romanians call the "long s" (it's written with a cedilla below it) is a mystery. But however we write the name no stretch of imagination can lead anyone to claim that Bucharest's an exciting city.

Its inhabitants used to claim it was the "Paris of the East". I think that referred mainly to the enormously wide boulevards built in imitation of Paris in the 19th century, when the country was finally freed from Turkish control. In part however the "Paris of the East" sobriquet reflected also the capital's burgeoning 19th century intellectual life, copied largely from Paris. Once released from Turkish control, Paris became every Romanian intellectual's Mecca, and French the language that every educated Romanian spoke. That remained true till the 1960s, and is partly so today.

Your first impression of Bucharest will be that it's dusty. That was the case long before the present spate of building made things so much worse. Your second will be that almost everything needs redecorating and/or renovating.

Fair enough. But if you stay long enough to begin to notice details you'll see that there are in fact a tremendous number of fine buildings that would look very impressive indeed were they properly maintained. Many are in the neo-classical idioms familiar to us. Some belong to what Romanians call Brincovenesc style, an extraordinary but very attractive mixture of oriental, gothic, baroque, and Venetian, introduced by Constantin Brincoveanu, Voivode of Wallachia (1688–1714: Chapter Thirteen). Too many – especially all the vast battery-stacking flats – are just horrors.

Many of the city's Orthodox churches are delightful. But even the Cathedral seems tiny to us, and all have different norms of church architecture from those we're accustomed to. When you've visited a few score you begin to appreciate their appeal, and to understand why Orthodox churchmen accuse the Western churches (they can't distinguish Wesleyans from Catholics any more than we can separate, say, Melkites from the Coptic Orthodox) of being "frightened of beauty".

Orthodox beauty lies in ornate details – the paintings of the saints on the iconostasis (literally "picture stand": it separates the body of the church from the "sanctuary" containing the altar), the icons and their frames, the frescos which may cover all or much of the church's interior, the polychrome texture, perhaps, of its exterior, the lights, the incense. There's little of the one-glance beauty of our own soaring

Cathedrals. That is as effectively lost on Orthodox eyes as Orthodox beauty is on ours – till we grow accustomed to it.

Bucharest's other un-obvious appeal is its parks. The ordinary tourist is apt to experience, especially in summer, endless dusty, hot streets. If you live there for a few weeks you begin to appreciate the greenery and lakes of centrally-placed Cismigiu, of Parcul Libertatii (Liberty Park) in the south, with its hyperbolic marble erection representing Liberty (from the Turks) and its vast, forlorn black marble mausoleum of the Communist leader Gheorghe Gheorghiu-Dej, still guarded by a lonely young sentry; Parcul Tineretului (Youth Park) just beyond it; the fine Botanical Gardens in the city's west; and Baneasa, Herastrau, Floreasca, and Tei Lakes in the north, all with adjoining parklands.

The parks all have lakes, which are in reality part of the innumerable streams flowing down from the Southern Carpathians across the swampy Danube plain to join the mighty river. The River Dimbovita, on whose banks Bucharest was planted and grew, has now almost disappeared, either underground or into a very unattractive concreted conduit.

Exploring Central Bucharest

How can you best explore this city which seems so determined to hide its attractions? I think your first move (as everywhere) is to orientate yourself on a few fixed points.

For Bucharest this is easy. The town's central area lies in an oval with the northern end at Piata Victoriei (Victory Square) and the southern at Piata Unirii (Unity Square). Very wide boulevards link the oval's two ends

and continue beyond them. Bulevardul Ana Ipatescu takes you south from Piata Victoriei as far as Piata Romana (Romanian Square). Bulevardul General Magheru and then Bulevardul N. Balcescu go as far as Piata Universatii and the Bulevardul Republicii crossroads. Bulevardul 1848 goes to Piata Unirii and the – at this point invisible – Dimbovita.

Today this is Bucharest's main axis. The much older, narrower, curving Calea Victoriei (Victory Avenue) also starts at Piata Victoriei, running in roughly the same direction. It ends at Piata Natiunile Unite (United Nations Square), actually over the Dîmbovita, eight or nine minutes walk northwest of Piata Unirii.

Much of what you'll want or need to see lies in or just off these two axes. The most important hotels, for instance, are here or nearby. The Inter-Continental towers not very appealingly over University Square. The Ambassador and Lido – dull facades both – almost face each other across Magheru Boulevard. The Dorobanti lies just east of Piata Romana in Calea Dorobantilor (Infantry Avenue; it commemorates infantry and local peasants who combined in a 1655 rebellion). The Athenee Palace, Bucharest's original attempt to answer London's Savoy, half-dominates Palace Square, through which the Calea Victoriei runs (the Square contains the former Royal Palace, scene of much of the December 1989 fighting). The hotel, hardly touched by gunfire, has the very attractive Atheneum concert hall in the gardens in front of it, the ruined National Gallery to its west across the square, and the burnt-out fine University Library a little to its south.

The northern end of the Calea Victoriei and streets off it form part of

Bucharest's embassy area. Fine old houses abound. One of the few city houses that have been fully renovated, an extremely ornate mansion, occupies the corner of Strada Biserica Amzei (Amzei Church Street) and Strada Cristian Tell. A century or so ago it was the home of a lady of slightly doubtful reputation – the first woman to ride a bicycle in Bucharest (enough to give any girl a bad name). You'll find Bucharest's best market (fruit, vegetables, delicatessen, drinks, etc) a little south of this house.

If you go straight across to Magheru Boulevard from here and turn south you soon have Strada Beloiannis almost opposite. Here, on the left, you'll see the HQ of the Automobil Clubul Roman (Romanian Automobile Club). They produce the best road map of Romania and the best street map of Bucharest, but don't distribute them very enthusiastically. The next turning off Magheru's same side is double – Strada Cosmonautilor and Strada Julles Michelet. The latter contains the British Embassy – on your right.

Back in Magheru, on the side opposite Julles Michelet and set back a little from the road, with car-parking in front, is a place you're almost certain to need to visit – the National Tourist Office (Oficiul National de Turism or ONT). It's often referred to as Carpati-ONT, and the office block above it houses the Ministry of Tourism, Carpati means, of course, Carpathians. The commercial, travel-agency-tour-operator side of the Ministry uses the name Carpati Tourist.

The combination of Ministry and commercial activities is confusing. It doesn't encourage efficiency, and in the past has done little for individual tourists, particularly those wanting information. Carpati Tourist-ONT-

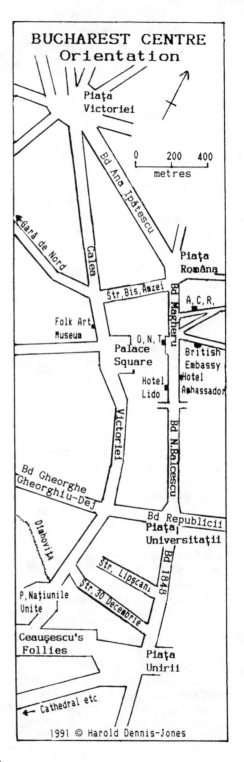

BUCHAREST CENTRE
Orientation

15

Ministry has seemed to concentrate on selling you package tours when you wanted to know the best way to see, say, wooden churches in the Salaj region or the opening hours of the Cluj Ethnographic Museum's Open Air section. And the staff (whose main job, after all, has been pleasing their bosses, not the public) has rarely appeared welcoming. As one frustrated traveller once commented to me: "These Romanians are unbelievably hospitable and helpful – unless they work in tourism". But I hope that will have changed by the time you read this.

Even if you don't want abstruse information this ONT office is a good place to change money. In summer allow time to queue.

Apart from the Atheneum already mentioned, most of Bucharest's theatres and concert halls can also be found in or close to the two main axes. These include the older Operetta Theatre, the Nottara Theatre, the Tanase Theatre, and others. The modern (1953) Opera House at 70 Bd. Gh. Gheorghiu-Dej, the westward continuation of the Bulevard Republicii, lies on the edge of our central oval. The large modern National Theatre stands beside the Inter-Continental Hotel, and the even vaster Hall of the Palace on Calea Victoriei's east side south of Palace Square (previously known as Republic Square and Gheorghe Gheorghiu-Dej Square: your maps may vary).

You'll find the main museums in this region too. The George Enescu Museum, commemorating the great Romanian composer-violinist, is housed in a fine neo-baroque mansion of 1900 at 141 Calea Victoriei. The superb National Folk Art Museum occupies another magnificent building (1906) at 107 Calea Victoriei. We've already noticed the National Art Collection housed in the former Royal Palace in Palace Square. No. 12 Calea Victoriei is a very striking vast building, completed in 1900 as Bucharest's General Post Office. It now houses a beautifully-displayed History of Romania Museum. After being filled in recent years with items relating to the dictator Ceausescu its future was a little undecided in 1990.

South of the Inter-Continental Hotel and University Square you'll find, to the west of the 1848 Boulevard, a tangle of streets that was the heart of Bucharest's original settlement. Though you can't actually see the river here today the town grew up on the low slope above it, and a very oriental character it must have had for much of its history, Strada Lipscani (Leipzigers' Street) today is lined with ordinary small shops. But it still possesses the feel and much of the look of a Near Eastern *souk*. It was named after the travelling Leipzig merchants who made it their base. Other nearby streets look like a souk too.

Their impact is strengthened by the Hanul lui Manuc (Manuc's Khan or Caravanserai) in Strada 30 Decembrie a little south of Strada Lipscani (don't confuse this with Strada 13 Decembrie, off Bulevardul N. Balcescu a good deal further north). The *khan* was built in oriental style early in the 19th century by an Armenian as a genuine caravanserai for travelling merchants, with large rooms where they could both sleep and store their wares.

Three storeys high and built round a spacious enclosed square it serves today mainly as a large open-air restaurant and beer cellar. But you can get a comfortable spacious room opening off one of the timbered balconies surrounding the courtyard if you wish. The hotel's cherished by Romanians mainly because the 1848 revolution was planned here.

In 30 December Street you can also see remains of the ancient palace (Princely Palace – Palatul Voievodal, or Curtea Veche – Old Court) that was home to the rulers of Wallachia after they'd moved from Tirgoviste in the Arges (Chapter Eleven), along with some other buildings. They are not very well maintained and there is little explanatory material, unfortunately. The church nearby, always called the Princely Church, is Bucharest's oldest.

If you continue southward you'll see a well-planted avenue going up a low slope on Piata Unirii's and the invisible Dimbovita's further side. At its top stands the little 17th century Orthodox Cathedral, with the Patriarch's small palace beyond it. The Cathedral is charming. But to enjoy it to the full you need to go there during the Sunday morning liturgy (I did this many years ago and became instantly hooked on Orthodox church chant, which has taken me into Orthodox churches in many countries and brought me many friends). Don't be afraid to wander in and out of Romanian churches like this. No one will mind. You won't be alone. Worshippers do it too. There are no seats. Provided you don't make a positive nuisance of yourself you can move about pretty freely. No one will think it odd.

The Patriarch's palace has jewels mounted on its inside walls. For many years the death penalty was retained in Romania only for the crime of pinching jewels from the inside walls of the Patriarch's palace and the outside walls of the palace occupied by the Metropolitan of Iasi (Chapter Six).

Romania's parliament building ("Palace of the Grand National Assembly") stands halfway up the little avenue, to the east. In old Communist days, although the building was used only a few days a year, the military prevented you from even walking near.

Before you're able to explore the avenue leading up to the Cathedral, however, you'll find yourself dazed by the gigantic expanse of Ceausescu's final megalomanic building spree, which you have to cross to reach the church. An enormous avenue, over a mile long and flanked by eight- and nine-storey flats, leads to the incredible eleven-storey Casa Republicii (Palace of the Republic).

The dictator had decided that all senior state officials should have offices in the Casa Republicii, and had reserved for himself a seven-room suite. Who exactly the thousands of flats were intended for isn't clear. Early in 1990 only a very tiny proportion were occupied. Work had stopped on the rest, with twenty tower cranes and heaven knows how many workers idle. Some time previously the architect had defected in desperation while on an official visit to West Germany.

Extraordinarily decorated central stone basins and fountains extend the length of the avenue, though these too are incomplete. Though all the structures are faced with elegant soft stone, and the buildings' design is very ornate, the incomplete portions make the work look decidedly shoddy. It's an amazing disaster, worth visiting for its sheer horror.

Nor are the Casa Republicii and the avenue the folly's only buildings. Some eight more vast office blocks surround the Casa, with more where the Calea Victoriei meets the Dimbovita at Piata Natiunile Unite.

17

One of Bucharest's most grandiose modern multiple stores, the Unirea, the earliest part of the redevelopment plan, occupies one side of Piata Unirii. It's worth wandering through to see the sort of things that purchasers queue for (you queue once to choose what you want and get a bill, once to pay, and once to collect your purchase) – and the things that planners have produced in profusion but no one wants.

One of Bucharest's best-loved Orthodox churches is tucked away to the avenue's north. Walk towards the massive Casa Republicii. Take the first turning on your right and you'll see the relatively large and certainly well-used Domnita (Princess) Balasa church. Its choir has the reputation of being better even than the Cathedral's. The present building is the fourth church on that site. Earlier structures crumbled because of the ground's swampiness.

Other centrally-placed churches which the Bucharest people love are the Cretulescu at 47 Calea Victoriei (1702) and the Stavreopolos (1730) at 4 Strada Postei. But there are lots of them, and they've never stopped serving their congregations since they were built, mostly several centuries ago. Not all the churches are worth spending time in. But don't hesitate to go into any that you're passing. On my last visit I discovered a tiny place that I thought was lovely. It stands at the top of some steps at the junction of Strada Gutenberg and Strada Silfidelor, between the Gheorghiu-Dej Boulevard and the Dimbovita near the Town Hall.

This is very much on the edge of our central oval. Bucharest's Town Hall stands nearby in Bulevardul Gheorghe Gheorghiu-Dej, almost opposite one corner of Cismigiu Park. At the bottom of Strada Brezoianu, going down towards the Dimbovita a little closer to Piata Unirri, you'll find the "Agentie CFR", the railway office where you buy tickets and make seat reservations for advance travel, and where you have to come for international tickets. It's in the same building as the national airline Tarom's booking office, and it's the Tarom sign that you'll notice in the street. The vast, stuffy, crowded railway booking office occupies the ground floor.

Off Centre

There are a number of places outside the central area that you'll probably want to see. One is the charming Botanical Gardens (Gradina Botanica). It lies a lot further west along the Gheorghiu-Dej Boulevard axis and then a few hundred metres northward up B-dul Dr Marinescu (note the standard abbreviation) and west to B-dul Controceni. You'll need a bus. But enquire first. The Gardens were reopened only in early 1990 after both they and B-dul Cotroceni had been closed because the Young Communists' vast centre to its south was planning expansion.

A more basic tourist haunt, the North Station (Gara de Nord), lies roughly west of Piata Victoriei. It's best reached along the Calea Grivitei, which joins Calea Victoriei opposite the already mentioned Strada Biserica Amzei and beside the National Folk Art Museum. From very early morning till very late at night the station itself is extremely crowded.

Train departures and arrivals are clearly shown on large boards. You can buy newspapers and the sorts of snacks common in Romania at lots of spots. In 1990 it was one of the few places in Bucharest where you could be certain of finding a licensed taxi – and lots of unlicensed ones. But there seemed to be no Tourist Information office, though there was a sign claiming to point to one.

If you want to buy a ticket for immediate travel you have to find the right booking window for your class and destination. If you're booking ahead – but only for destinations inside Romania – go to the new "agentie" in the square south of the station's frontage, near the Hotel Nord. Allow plenty of time for queueing – maybe twice if you pick the wrong window first time round.

Almost everyone will want to see the Village Museum (Museul Satului) on the shores of Lake Herastrau in the park of the same name (No. 331 bus from Piata Romana). Its entrance lies in Soseaua (= la Chaussee) Kiseleff, the most grandiose of all Bucharest's avenues. This starts at Piata Victoriei and runs NNW in a straight line past the Triumphal Arch, built to celebrate the Romanian Army's victory in WWI (Chapter Twelve), to the Scinteia building (Casa Scinteii), Communist Bucharest's outstanding monstrosity till Ceausescu's recent excesses.

It's a huge tall structure with what can only be called a phallic emblem on top (Ceausescu's Casa Republicii has something very similar, but smaller). Built to celebrate the "achievements of the National Economy" (I quote a Romanian English-language guidebook), it houses the Council of Culture and Socialist Education and what was the editorial offices of the Communist Party newspaper *Scinteia* ("knowledge").

The statue of Lenin in Piata Scinteii was removed early in 1990 after a huge struggle to uproot it.

Kiseleff Avenue is leafy and pleasant. It was named in honour of a popular Russian Governor of Romania, appointed by the Turks after the Russo-Turkish War of 1828-29. The fine houses lining it constitute what everyone calls the "*nomenklatura* district", set aside for senior Party officials. The entrance to the Village Museum lies to your right not far beyond the Triumphal Arch.

The Village Museum is one of the world's largest and most famous open-air museums. It contains scores of traditional buildings from every part of Romania, every one of them appropriately furnished with its region's handicraft products. Many of these are priceless because of their age. The collection covers 25 leafy hectares and there's a separate museum building. It would be absurd to visit Bucharest without going to the Village Museum. But if you want to digest what the museum displays you'll need to stay at least several weeks.

There's a smaller and much more manageable collection in this area that illustrates some aspects of Romanian handicrafts – the Dr N. Minovici Museum of Folk Art, at 1 Minovici Street, off Soseaua Baneasa close to the Baneasa Station. It's well worth a visit. Soseaua Baneasa leads almost due north from Piata Scinteii towards Bucharest's Otopeni Airport and Ploiesti. Baneasa Station was built for the royal family and is now used for tourist excursion trains.

Rather further afield, 14 km from central Bucharest, you can enjoy another collection of typical Romanian products at Mogosoaia Palace. This was built by Constantin Brincoveanu himself in 1702. The building (in florid Brincovenesc style – see Chapter Twelve) is magnificent. So are its contents – silverware, sculptures, gold and silver embroideries, rare books, and much else. So too is the park surrounding the Palace and its cool, peaceful lake.

The Palace lies on the DNIA road to Ploiesti (DN equals Drum National, national route). If you're driving, leave Bucharest by Calea Grivitei (the old DN7, not the modern motorway to Pitesti) and take the well-signposted turning to Mogosoaia. If you're without a car it's worth taking a coach tour.

Accommodation in Bucharest

I've mentioned the main hotels in Bucharest's central area. Also the only one outside it – the Nord. Lesser hotels are almost all inside this part of the town. Private-house accommodation, when it gets under way again, is likely to be fairly central because no modern suburban flats are large enough to have guest rooms. If you take private-house accommodation you'll not be able to rely on taxis and will have to learn to cope with the crowded buses, trams, and Metro.

At the moment there are no campsites within really easy reach of the city's centre. This is something that needs attention. There are however campsites in the outer suburbs, such as Snagov (40 km out, on DN1). Snagov, with its lake and forest, is itself a minor tourist centre. But it's a bit distant from central Bucharest.

Getting Around

Using your own car is very difficult, especially in the centre's tangled narrow streets unless you know the city well. Convenient parking-places rarely exist. Walking becomes unbearably hot and sticky in summer. And anyway the distances are too great even for a determined pedestrian like myself. Whether you like it or not you're liable to have to learn to cope with the Metro and the buses and trams. Arm yourself with suitable bus/tram tickets and a pocket or purse full of 1 leu coins.

The Metro's basic layout is fairly simple – a north-south line following the main boulevards' axis from beyond Piata Victoriei to a long way past Piata Unirii, with ring lines intersecting the main-axis route at Victoriei and Unirii and one spur off this ring.

Few maps are available to the public. Even worse, the maps in dimly-lit stations and on trains are triumphs of illegibility. You have to peer at them closely to read the names. To add to problems station names are scarce and inconspicuous on ill-lit station platforms. The first few journeys are hell. But one learns to cope.

There's no map available for surface transport either. And buses and trams are, if anything, more crowded during the day than the Metro. But, again, one learns to cope – at least with regular journeys.

To help you, there's a specially-drawn Metro map on p. 114.

5. The Black Sea Coast

If you go by train from Bucharest to the main Black Sea town and port of Constanta the distance is 225 km, and the time taken about four hours. The spelling Constantza is often used outside Romania to represent the sound of the Romanian "long t" (*t* with a cedilla below it). But you won't normally see the *-tz-* in Romanian-language signs. In Romanian the Black Sea is called *Marea Neagra*.

Once you've left the capital's suburbs the railway runs in an almost straight line for 130 km till just northwest of Fetesti, where it's joined by the main line coming from Suceava (Chapter Six) and points beyond in Poland and the USSR, such as Lvov, Moscow, and Warsaw. Just beyond Fetesti the linked route crosses the Danube's arms and its miles of floodlands to Cernavoda by the 17-kilometer-long Cernavoda Bridge, Europe's longest when built in 1895. Beyond Cernavoda, at Medgidia, the line divides. The more southerly branch runs inland southward to the Bulgarian Black Sea port of Varna. The more westerly serves Constanta, Romania's main outlet on the Black Sea, and point south to Mangalia. A third line comes in at Medgidia from the north, from the Danube Delta port of Tulcea.

The Cernavoda bridge was brand new when Stoker wrote *Dracula*. At the end of the book the hero Jonathan Harker makes his final return across this bridge by train from Varna.

However much he distorted historical facts Stoker certainly researched his horror tale very effectively.

If you travel by road between Bucharest and Constanta you cover 270-odd kilometres and take a lot longer. You have to go northwest out of Bucharest on the DN2 (the main road to Moldavia) and turn east onto the DN2A at Urziceni. On this route you go through Slobozia, a dull town, and see another spectacular structure – the huge, attractively humped, modern, four-lane suspension bridge 1.5 km long crossing the Danube at its only single-channel point close to Giurgeni. Half the bridge's length has the Danube's waters below it.

However impressed you may be by these bridges, bear in mind that photographing bridges is still illegal in Romania.

Until you reach the Danube there's nothing much on either route to attract your attention – except perhaps the huge balanced-arm draw wells traditional on the Danube Plain and the miles and miles of maize or sunflowers or other crops.

Beyond the Danube you come to the rolling hills and low plateau land of the Dobrogea. Filled with vast fields of sunflowers, other crops, woods, and vineyards, this, roughly speaking, is the rectangle of land between the Danube and the Black Sea where the river turns north for a time before turning eastward again into its extraordinary delta. Dobrogea is the Romanian spelling. The Slav spelling Dobrudja however is often used because of Bulgaria's influence in the region.

After being in Turkish hands for several centuries, Romania's rights were recognised at the Congress of Berlin in 1878 (Chapter Twelve) and the boundary pushed further south than it now is. One result is that a decidedly whimsical pseudo-oriental summer palace built for the Romanian royal family on the Black Sea coast at Balcic (or, if you prefer, Baltchik) is now in Bulgaria. You can visit it on coach excusions from Romanian Black sea resorts.

The Dobrogea today is a peaceful fertile area. It contains several good wine-producing regions, such as Murfatlar, another excursion destination for holidaymakers from the coast, as well as Romania's only nuclear power station (near Cernavoda). The recently-completed Danube Canal cuts across it, from Agigea, just south of Constanta to near Cernavoda. It shortens considerably the upstream distance to the Danube's inland harbours for sea-going vessels, and saves them also the difficulties of navigating through the Delta, described below.

You can fly in about an hour direct from Bucharest to Constanta.

Constanta

Constanta's a bustling harbour and industrial city of nearly a quarter of a million inhabitants today. But it has a history that goes back to ancient Greek legends. Its Greek, and later Roman, name was Tomi, a word meaning "sections" or "slices" (it's our words "tomes"). It was connected with Jason's and his Argonauts' search for the Golden Fleece, and with the story of Medea. Pursued at sea by her father Aeetes, King of Colchis, whom she was trying to escape from, she cut her small brother into pieces and threw them into the sea. Dad stopped to pick the pieces up and give them proper burial on land. Medea escaped.

More factually, we know that the trading settlement of Tomi was founded by emigrants from Miletus who had settled on the present-day Turkish coast in the 6th century BC. For centuries it prospered. The Roman Empire's ever-widening spread brought it under Roman control five hundred years later.

It became famous down to our own days as the place the great Roman poet Ovid was banished to in AD 9 because of his relationship with the Emperor Augustus's daughter Livia. He wrote his *Tristia* (Sorrows) and his *Epistulœ ex Ponto* (Letters from the Black Sea) in Tomi. His poetry exercised enormous influence over a vast number of later European writers. The *Tristia* and the *Epistulœ ex Ponto* formed part of almost every well-educated person's reading till just after the end of WWII. Romanians are naturally rather proud that Ovid praised local hospitality considerably.

In the 4th century AD, when the Roman Empire was falling apart, Tomi came under Byzantium's (Constantinople's) rule and was known as Constantiana. When the Byzantine Empire in its turn began to crumble the Genoese moved in for a century or more. But after the fall of Constantinople in 1453 the Turks moved north and took over. Their rule lasted until 1878. A small Turkish minority still survives here.

One result of all this is that in Constanta you can see a fine modern statue of the poet Ovid; the remains of an obviously prosperous and important Roman building with a magnificent mosaic pavement from the 3rd century AD (magnificently preserved and presented, too); other Greek and Roman remains; a mosque and an Orthodox cathedral in the same street, the Strada Muzeelor (Museums' Street), which contains good Archaeological and Arts Museums; a Catholic church nearby; and a Genoese lighthouse – all in the same small area on the peninsula between the inner commercial harbour and the yacht harbour facing the open sea.

Close to Ovid's statue in the Piata Ovidiu, also known as Piata Independentei, there's a Greek Orthodox church, a reminder of the Greek traders who settled here in the later days of Turkish rule, and a somewhat ornate, partly Brincovenesc (Chapter Twelve) Town Hall dating from 1921. An excellent aquarium, displaying some 4500 species from the Black Sea, the Danube, and Romania's lakes, faces a modern Casino which looks out onto the sea itself in B-dul 16 Februarie, on the peninsula's southern side. The fact that the main Roman remains are located directly above the commercial port somehow gives you a good idea of what the town must have looked like in Roman times.

If you arrive by train you can reach this part of the town by bearing slightly left (there's a choice of parallel streets) while walking directly away from the station. The airport lies north of the town. In high season excursions operate from here to places such as Kiev and Istambul, in addition to year-round flights to Bucharest. Trips along the coast by boat are also laid on in summer. Though Constanta itself isn't really a tourist resort it has a pleasant, wide beach. The town's two first-category hotels cater primarily for business visitors.

Mamaia

Mamaia, 12 km north of Constanta, is Romania's main sea resort. It's an almost purely modern settlement, with some sixty hotels, restaurants, shops, very attractively planted gardens, several swimming pools, including one of Olympic size, first-aid posts, nightclubs and discos, bars, an open-air theatre, and everything else summer visitors can possibly need – all laid out on a sandbar some 15 km long, but only 150-400 m wide, separating the sea from a sweetwater lagoon called Lake Siutghiol. The beach on the seaward side, composed of fine shell-sand with occasional tamarisk bushes, slopes gently into the sea – a little too gently for some enthusiastic swimmers. It's wide for a good 8 km, so that despite your thousands of fellow-holidaymakers you never feel jostled.

Before 1960 there were very few buildings on the sandbar. Almost the only ones remaining from previous days are a small mosque and a mansion where the royal family entertained summer guests. This has now been converted into the de luxe International Hotel.

The resort was very carefully planned. It began to take shape in the early 1960s and was fully operative by about 1966. Since then the trees, shrubs, and flowers from the early days have matured, and a lot more hotels, restaurants, and shops have been built. Full use is made of Lake Siutghiol for watersports of every sort – canoeing, sailing (dinghies can be hired), water-skiing, board-sailing, and so on. The island in the lake has been re-named Ovidiu (what else? there's a village with that name inland from the lake) and a restaurant of reed-covered huts built on it which specialises in fish dishes typical of the Dobrogea and Danube Delta.

Summer at Mamaia, from mid-June to early September, can be very hot indeed. The air temperature averages 22°C and the sea temperature 17°C. The sun blazes down for up to 14 hours a day, and cloudy days are rare. At this time of year the resort's only disadvantage is the distance from one end to the other. It's not the sort of stretch anyone's much inclined to walk. Trolleybuses run up and down the main road, but you still sometimes find yourself needing to walk a bit. Outside high season Mamaia's pretty bleak and often decidedly cold.

All sorts of excursions are run regularly from here. You can go by coach to all the spots described in this chapter, though the amount of exploration you can do in a day in the Danube Delta is obviously limited. You can have a look at Balcic in Bulgaria and some of Bulgaria's well-planned sea resorts. You can go by train or plane to Bucharest for the day, or fly to Suceava to visit the "Painted Churches" (Chapter Six). Or fly for a couple of days to Kiev, the USSR's Crimean resorts, or Istambul. Longer sea trips to Istambul are also sometimes organised.

Holidaymakers of all nationalities, East European as well as Western, flock to Mamaia. It's rather a pity that differences in tastes, language, and spending power have made the Romanians decide that certain hotels need to be earmarked for certain nationalities. The only one where I've experienced mixing is the International, which is expensive.

If you buy a package to Mamaia you'll find yourself in a hotel where the cooking won't offend any Brit, the facilities match those in other holiday countries, and all, or nearly all, the staff speak at least a little English.

Trolleybuses run frequently into Constanta. The distance from the resort's southern edge is about 5 km. The Parc Hotel at this end of the town is the excursion coaches' last departure point and sometimes used as pick-up spot for specialised trips with fewer participants.

Romanians and others who want an inexpensive holiday with access to all Mamaia's facilities find themselves private rooms in Mamaia Sat (Mamaia Village) a little to the north. There are well-equipped campsites north and south of the resort. Navodari, north of Mamaia Sat, has been developed as a schoolchildren's resort. You'll find camping "bungalows" there.

The Other Black Sea Resorts

The first settlement south of Constanta, Agigea, isn't strictly speaking a resort, though it has a tuberculosis sanatorium. It's also the site of a biological research station dealing with the Black Sea and of a small Nature Reserve on the dunes 50 m from the sea which shelters rare fauna and flora. The Danube Canal joins the sea here.

Agigea lies 10 km south of Constanta. Eforie Nord, 4 km beyond it, is half resort and half health spa. Its 4-km-long beach is about 20 m wide, and is backed by wooded land on a ridge rising 20-25 m above the sea. Apart from a considerable number of normal tourist hotels, restaurants, bars, discos, open-air cinemas, and a fine large park, it boasts also a vast artificial seawater lake, together with several sanatoria handling various ailments. A special treatment said to be extremely efficacious depends on your being covered with black mud from Lake Techirghiol, lying a little south.

Eforie Sud (South Eforie) is, in effect a smaller continuation, some 4 km away, of Eforie Norde. From 25 m above sea level the land here descends to a height of a mere 7-8 m towards Lake Techirghiol, which was originally a sea gulf. Thanks to evaporation its water is six times as saline as the sea and its mud is credited with many healing properties. Various Romanian doctors have devised treatments to delay ageing, using medicaments such as Gerovital, and Eforie has become a world centre for their application.

The village of Techirghiol lies at the lake's edge. Apart from more treatment centres there's a 16th century wooden church here, built without any metal and brought from Transylvania in the 1930s. Very appealing heads of a monk and a nun are carved on one of its doorposts.

Tuzla, 21 km from Constanta, is a fishing village built on the site of a Roman settlement. Costinesti, 7 km beyond it, has a sheltered beach 3 km long and 100 m wide. It has been developed as Romania's youth holiday centre. All students are entitled to 12 days free holiday at Costinesti. Just beyond Costinesti you come to the little village named 23 August, with another former sea-gulf inland and a small beach.

Another 8 km brings you to the outskirts of a well-developed resort area usually collectively called Neptun, though it's technically divided north to south into Olimp, Neptun and Jupiter. Like Mamaia, this is another wholly modern resort area. It has been developed in the Comorova Forest's luxuriant vegetation inland of three sweetwater lakes, two of them re-named Neptun and Jupiter, with the much smaller Tismana to their south.

A number of hotels in this area are used by British tour operators. I think their clients appreciate the shade that Neptun's wooded land provides and its relatively peaceful atmosphere. But the resort's also well equipped for less affluent holidaymakers. It has good ordinary campsites and also one with a number of small chalets, always referred to as "bungalows". Apart from the normal restaurants, shops, bars, discos, etc Neptun possesses a children's recreation park called Prichindel (Tom Thumb), a sports ground, and water sports facilities on its lakes. As in Mamaia, some of the restaurants offer floorshows. There is of course a good selection of excursions available.

Cap Aurora, sometimes treated as a separate resort, lies south of Neptun, with a vast hotel of unusual design above the cape's tip. Another small modern resort, Venus, lies directly beyond the cape. Olimp-Neptun-Jupiter-Cap Aurora-Venus stretch over a bare 4 km. Treating them as a single locality seems natural enough.

Saturn's the last of this string of modern resorts. Apart from several hotels it too posseses a campsite, with "bungalows" available at a very reasonable price.

Immediately beyond Saturn you reach the harbour town of Mangalia, which claims to have more of a Mediterranean climate than spots further north. Spring, they say, comes earlier and autumn later. The site first appears in history as the ancient Greek trading station Callatis. It kept that name under the Romans and Byzantines, but became Pangalia when taken over by the Genoese in the 13th century. Dubrovnik traders, however, who travelled overland as well as by sea throughout the Mediterranean world from their Yugoslav Adriatic base knew it as Mangalia.

Mangalia is fundamentally still a fishing harbour and small commercial port. But it has a pleasant wide beach, 3 km long, and several very acceptable hotels, as well as a number of sanatoria and treatment centres. You can see remains of the old citadel walls, uncovered in 1960, and a small archaeological museum. The mosque dates from 1590.

All that remains now before you reach the Bulgarian frontier is the tiny fishermen's village called 2 Mai (2 May), 2 km from Mangalia, and the frontier town appropriately named Vama Veche (Old Customs Post – Vama is one of Romanian's many words borrowed from Turkish). The distance from Mangalia is 7 km.

From Constanta to Mangalia the main DN39 runs inland. If you've driven down the coast looking at all these resort areas you can return very quickly. Making an excursion by road from anywhere on the coast into Bulgaria is also very speedy thanks to the DN39. But if you make a Bulgarian excursion on your own remember that you'll probably need a Bulgarian visa (consult your hotel or campsite). Coach excursionists go in and out of that country without trouble.

North to the Danube Delta

The region between Mamaia's northern suburbs and the Danube Delta contains some of Romania's least known and least visited spots.

Babadag is almost the only real town in the 70 miles separating Mamaia and Tulcea, the town at the delta's base and the river's port nearest the sea. Tulcea's industrialised today. But it was in Turkish hands from the 14th century on, and still possesses a 14th century mosque and fountain. The countryside round both Babadag and Tulcea today produces good wine. But one of Romania's most impressive archaeological sites also lies off the DN22 road linking Constanta to Tulcea. It's the ancient Greek city of Histria.

If you turn east roughly 50 km from Constanta you later pass on your left a turning to the village of Istria. The ruins of Histria lie some 10 km beyond the turning. It was founded by Greeks from Miletus in the 7th century BC and today contains ruins of buildings constructed between the 5th century BC and 6th century AD.

The most notable items include a 5th century BC temple of Aphrodite, houses, baths, and temples up to the 1st century BC, defensive walls and towers built by the Romans on very solid Greek foundations after the Goths had destroyed much of the town in the 3rd century AD, Roman baths from the 3rd century AD, a large basilica in the central square (5th century AD), and shops and workshops of a century later, together with related sculpture, pottery, inscriptions, and mosaics.

For many centuries Histria looked out from its promontory over open sea. But all the approaches to its harbour were silted up by sand which the Danube spilled out into the Black Sea. Merchants transferred their trade to Tomi. Today a long sandbar has formed a series of lagoons northward along the coast from just south of ancient Histria. They've been given the names of Lakes Sinoe, Smoica, Golovita, and vast Razelm. Only two openings connect sea and lagoons.

It's a lonely area, with very few roads. But it's rich in fish. For the most part the lagoons are barely a metre deep. In places however this increases to 3 metres. The region's chief fish-handling centre is just outside Unirea, formerly Jurilovca, reached by a turning off the DN22 roughly 75 km north of Constanta. Unirea itself is one of the main settlements inhabited by Lipovani, descendants of heretic refugees from Russian persecution who settled beside Lake Razelm and in the Romanian part of the Danube Delta in the late 18th century, bringing their customs and culture with them.

There's a late 19th century Lipovan house from Unirea/Jurilovca in the Village Museum in Bucharest. It's of typical wooden plank construction, decorated inside with mural oil paintings, especially on the ceilings, and a bread oven and steam bath very similar to our modern saunas in the garden. Chanting in the Lipovan churches is reputedly magnificent.

A rough track leads northwest from Unirea to the remains of another ancient Greek settlement, known by its Roman name of Argamnum, and north from there to the late Byzantine fortress of Heraclea, built to keep out the 7th century's many invaders. From Hereaclea you can turn west to Babadag.

The items I've mentioned aren't the only points of interest to travellers. The whole way of life of the fisherfolk in this northern part of the Dobrogea is fascinating. But to know it properly you need to stay weeks in the area and to speak the language – or have someone with you who does.

A pleasant campsite, set in a wood just south of Babadag, makes a good exploring base. If you're merely passing through, you'll find restaurants in the town itself. Regular buses connect Constanta with Tulcea. On the train you travel via Medgidia.

The Danube Delta

Tulcea, at almost exactly the Delta's innermost point, is your starting-point for all Delta travel. It's an ancient town, settled like Constanta by Greeks from Miletus in the 7th century BC under the name Aegyssus, which it still had in Ovid's day. When Aegyssus was founded the Delta as we see it today hardly existed. The Danube's mouth was mainly a broad estuary with a Greek trading station on its bank. We know that because Herodotus, "the father of history", visited and described it in about 450 BC. All sorts of invaders and their armies have passed through since then. The last were the Turks, who kept a tight grip on Romania's Black Sea coastal strip.

As a result, despite modern factories and much modern building, you can still see corners that reflect its oriental past. There's a 19th century mosque, for instance. The building which attracts most attention from visitors, however, is the fine modern Aquarium and Danube Delta Museum. The Aquarium, in the basement, contains specimens of the hundred-odd fish species found in the Danube, including some of the rarest. The most popular exhibit in the Museum is the 13th century Tatar Treasure consisting mainly of silver ingots and gold Byzantine coins, along with some Tatar khans' (chieftains') seals.

There's another, smaller archaeological museum at the foot of a hill to the town's northeast, known as Horea's Hill (Colnicul Horei) because of the monument to the leader of the 1784 revolt (Chapter Twelve) on its summit. Apart from fish refrigeration plant the town also has several wineries. The harbour faces a wide stretch of water, where ships can turn and dock, with a smaller yacht harbour and passenger-boat base close to it.

If you're a bit short-sighted and wonder why a lot of people standing dead still on the quayside are staring into the sky, it will probably be because a huge flock of pelicans is flying overhead. They make an amazing sight. The pelicans fly in a constantly-changing V-formation, wheeling and dipping, breaking and re-forming. You can watch them for hours. They provide a very effective introduction to the Delta's amazing wildlife, mostly still thriving despite inescapable modern pollution and some mistaken efforts at commercialisation and industrialisation.

The pelicans, both white and Dalmatian, arrive in April-May and leave in October. Their breeding-grounds, notably around the open water known as Lake Matita, are strictly-protected Nature Reserves.

But pelicans are a long way from being the Delta's only rare birds. Over three hundred species in all are regularly identified here, some of them rare and many not found in Western Europe. They include the black vulture, Egyptian vulture, pygmy cormorant, great white egret, black-winged stilt, roller, great bustard, and a range of herons.

Plants, fish, and other animals display the same variety. Remains of old oak forests exist alongside willow, poplar,

ash, wild cherry, hops, and vines. Huge creepers hanging from oaks at Letea and elsewhere resemble a tropical mangrove swamp, especially when the river level is high and the ground flooded.

Among the plants white water-lilies are the most noticeable and best-loved. But you'll find yellow irises, water mint, bulrushes, sedges, water docks, and a huge host of other aquatic plants. Two insect-eaters are among the rarer varieties. Carp predominate among the fish (in Romanian they're called *crap*), and the most valuable is the sturgeon, now unfortunately far less numerous than once they were. There are a fair number of not-too-poisonous snakes as well.

Despite all this variety the scene that predominates in the Delta is simply miles and miles of reeds, with the rhizomes that act as roots knotted together to form large and small floating islands. Nothing in the Delta is static – that's part of its appeal. The whole land-mass is anyway advancing into the Black Sea at several metres a year. When you've fought your way in a small boat through some seemingly well-marked channel you're quite likely to find your route blocked by a huge floating reed-island when you try to return. Today the reeds are commercially harvested, in some places on a very large scale. Their chemical composition makes them valuable in paper production and for many other purposes.

Only one-seventh of the delta's 434,000 ha consists of land, and some of that is liable to flooding. This naturally affects the way you travel. The river's main flow is channelled into three arms – the Chilia Arm (Bratul Chilia) in the north, much of it forming the frontier with the USSR,

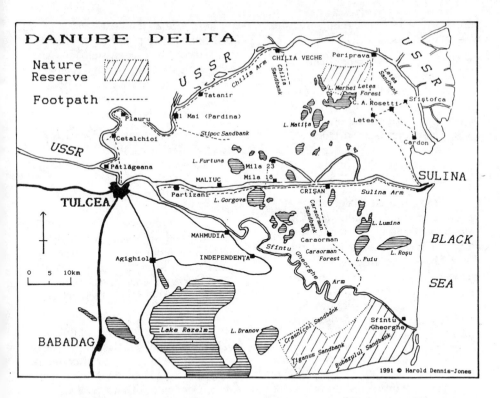

DANUBE DELTA

Nature Reserve [hatched]

Footpath -------

USSR

CHILIA VECHE Periprava
USSR
Chilia Arm
Chilia Sandbank
L. Merhei Letea Forest
Tatanir
Letea Sandbank
Sfiştofca
C. A. Rosetti
Plauru
1 Mai (Pardina)
L. Matita Letea
Cetalchioi
Stipoc Sandbank
Cardon
USSR
L. Furtuna
SULINA
Pătlăgeana
Mila 23
L. Furtuna
MALIUC Mila 18
TULCEA
Partizani CRIŞAN Sulina Arm
L. Gorgova
Caraorman Sandbank
L. Lumina
MAHMUDIA Caraorman
BLACK
Agighiol
INDEPENDENŢA
Sfîntu Caraorman Forest
L. Roşu
Gheorghe L. Puiu
0 5 10km
Arm
SEA
Lake Razelm L. Dranov
Crasnicol Sandbank
Sfîntu Gheorghe
BABADAG
Tiganus Sandbank
Bubazuiul Sandbank

1991 © Harold Dennis-Jones

the central Sulina Arm, which has been widened and straightened for sea-going vessels, and the winding, tortuous St George Arm (Bratul Sfintu Gheorghe) to the south, with a number of cleared channels that connect it to Lake Razelm (or Razim) and its linked lagoons. The land on each side of the three main arms is solid all the way to the sea, except at the many points where channels branch from the major waterways.

It you take a day-trip excursion to the Delta you're unlikely to see more of it than the main Sulina Arm as far as Maliuc and back. It doesn't give you much idea of the floating reed-bed *plaur* scenery, nor of what a *grind* (sandbank formed from silt brought down by the river) can look like. To do that you'll need to make your base somewhere in the Delta area; ensure that you have adequate information

about accommodation, scheduled boat services, and footpaths; and then explore by boat and on foot – unless, of course, your Romanian is fluent enough for you to persuade local people who know the region really well to take you through some of its remoter corners in their boats. The Tourist Office at Tulcea is the place at which to make planning enquiries.

There are hotels at Maliuc on the Sulina Arm's northern bank some 15 km from Tulcea; at Crisan on the southern bank some 11 km beyond Maliuc; and at Sulina, on the southern bank right at the Danube's mouth, another 13 km away. The one at Sulina is the best equipped. You can reach all these points by regular slow and fast boat services between Tulcea and Sulina. You can travel also to Mila 23, a small settlement on a loop of the Danube's original central channel that

29

was shortened when the Sulina Arm was straightened.

On the Chilia Arm boat services operate as far as Periprava, 25 km from the sea and the point at which a sub-delta lying wholly in the USSR begins to fan out on the opposite bank. The distance from Tulcea to Sulina is 71 km, to Periprava 103. To reach Sfintu Gheorghe on the St George Arm you cover 118 km.

Fairly simple tourist chalets exist at various points in the delta. But they belong mostly to private concerns, and you'll have to ask about using them. There's a campsite at Crisan, halfway along the Sulina Arm, one near Tulcea, and one, reached by a normal road, at Independenta, beside the St George Arm a little less than half way to the sea.

If you want a proper view of the Delta – and it's well worth having – you must juggle your accommodation with boat arrival and departure times and with your own walking speed and capacity. If you camp at Tulcea (or stay in the comfortable Delta or Egreta hotels) you can probably catch the earliest possible fast boat to Sulina, explore the little town and relax briefly, walk the 10 km or so to Letea via the smaller settlement of Cardon, and then either return to Sulina before the last boat returns to Tulcea or continue another 8 km or so to Periprava and catch a boat from there. If you're less energetic you might like to walk only as far as Cardon, or just a little beyond (about 5 km), and then go back to Sulina. There are no hills to contend with. But you can't be certain the going underfoot will always be too solid. Find out everything you can beforehand in Tulcea.

There are other paths linking settlements along the Sulina Arm's southern side all the way from Partizani, first stop on the slow boats from Tulcea, to Sulina itself. This isn't particularly exciting. From Crisan however it's not more than an hour's walk southward to Caraorman, set in a forest rather similar to Letea's.

The other main paths connect Tulcea's Tudor Vladimirescu suburb (the Romanians have a habit of re-naming towns and villages after famous men associated with them – for Vladimirescu see Chapter Twelve) with Pardina, now re-named I Mai, some 40 km away, and with Chilia Veche, a further 35 km out along the Chilia Arm. From a few kilometres short of Pardina a path follows the Stipoc Grind about 20 km to Batacu village.

That can be an awful lot of walking for one day, however well you fit in your boat travel. All of which means that you may have to think about camping wild or perhaps sleeping in the open. Any walking in the Delta involves carrying food and drink for the day and, in summer, from mid-May till about October, protecting yourself against ferocious midges. If you plan to camp or sleep out make sure you have an effective mosquito net. Merely zipping up the tent is useless. The local authorities insist on you taking rubber boots, a torch, knife, and basic first-aid. To avoid fire I'd suggest not even taking matches with you, and abandoning cigarettes and hot food for the day. But consult the Tulcea Tourist Office.

A lot of effort? Yes, but well worth it. Apart from the wildlife and the scenic interest you'll also inevitably learn a little about the life of the hardy people who inhabit the Delta. For centuries they lived as best they could by catching fish and selling them to anyone who would buy them. After WWII fishery stations were established which bought their catches and guaranteed them minimum monthly payments whatever the quantity of fish delivered. Most of them today have motor-powered vessels.

You can hire guides and boats at places such as Maliuc and Crisan if you want to explore the Delta's watery wilds. So aim to stay also at one of these places. Picking a spot on the St George Arm avoids the main tourist stream.

Inland Dobrogea

There are three major points of tourist interest inland from the Dobrogea's coast – Murfatlar, Adamclisi, and the Danube Canal.

Murfatlar, 18 km inland due west of Constanta on the DN3, is a favourite excursion destination with coastal holidaymakers, mainly because of the fine wines produced in the region and the excuse a trip to the winery offers of sampling its products, along with a good dinner and maybe a doze in the homeward-bound coach. Murfatlar wines are indeed good, with plenty of body and a mass of international awards from past years. But this is only one of Romania's worthwhile wine regions.

Nor is the winery Murfatlar's only attraction. Much nearby countryside is also very pleasantly wooded. Just south of Murfatlar vilage the Fintinita-Murfatlar Nature Reserve, rarely more than 100m wide, stretches for a considerable distance over the steep, wooded slopes of some limestone hills, covering an area of 66 ha in all. Its trees and extremely varied grassy vegetation include many species rare in Romania, in a setting that's unique.

The village of Basarabi, which forms part of Murfatlar commune, contains even stranger remains. Some time ago

it was discovered that three small Christian churches, one above the other, had been cut into a limestone hill. Tools, Glagolitic inscriptions, pottery, and mural drawings were also found. While many items suggested a 10th century date there were also indications that the earliest of the churches might go back to Roman times, suggesting the existence of Christianity – perhaps among Roman troops or traders – long before the 9th century journeys of St Cyril and St Methodius and their followers resulted in the country's more complete Christianisation.

No doubts are possible about the date of the Tropaeum Trajani (Trajan's Victory Trophy) 2 km from the village of Adamclisi (64 km from Constanta, continuing on the DN3 beyond Murfatlar). It was built in AD 109 to celebrate the Roman Emperor Trajan's victory over the Dacians (Chapter Twelve). In shape it's nearly circular. It's main feature is a series of 54 bas-reliefs consisting of six groups of nine scenes each.

While the bas-reliefs on Trajan's Column, erected in Rome, with copies in Carthage and Byzantium, tell the entire story of Trajan's Dacian campaign, the Tropaeum displays more stylised representation of the fighting. In each group there's a scene of marching, a battle scene, and a scene of surrender. The Emperor himself appears in every group.

A mausoleum which contains bodies of Roman soldiers stands a little north of the Tropaeum. The remains of a small fortified town founded by Trajan after the battle and similarly named Tropaeum Trajani lie nearly 2 km south and 1 km west of Adamclisi village.

The Danube Canal is wholly modern.

It came into use only in the later 1980s. Its purpose was to shorten the distance and difficulty for sea-going vessels intending to sail up the Danube of navigating through the Delta and up the Danube's main inland channel. It cuts through the countryside from Agigea, immediately south of Constanta, to the Danube close to Cernavoda.

While there's nothing particularly spectacular about the Danube Canal the two-day trips aboard comfortable, relatively small passenger vessels offer all the restfulness of water-borne travel along with a chance to see some of the Dobrogea's pleasant peaceful scenery. As is traditional aboard cruising vessels, the food is excellent.

If you're driving in the Dobrogea's northern parts, you may like to see the tiny, early 4th century crypt church discovered fairly recently at Niculitel, about 3 km south of the DN22 30 km west of Tulcea on the way to Galati (next chapter). An 18th century mosque has survived at Macin on the same road, 13 km from Braila, 85 from Tulcea.

Strada Lipscani (Leipzigers Street),
in Bucharest's old centre, still has
the atmosphere of an Oriental souk.

In Sibiu (Hermannstadt), the
Fingerling Ladder connects
Upper and Lower towns.

The fine Princely Church at
Tîrgoviște stands beside the
palace ruins in one of medieval
Wallachia's capitals.

Agapia Monastery in Moldavia, surrounded by nuns' dwellings, was founded in 1447, and rebuilt in 1823 after being burnt by Turks.

6. Moldavia

Moldavia (Moldova in Romanian and many other languages) emerged as a separate territorial entity in mid-14th century. But while its western boundary has always been clearly marked by the Eastern Carpathians' crests, its northern, eastern, and southern limits have varied. In 1812, for instance, after the Russo-Turkish war of 1806–07, when the Russians were pushing south in efforts to take over as much of the Turks' decaying empire as they could, the Peace of Bucharest (made between Turks and Russians; the Romanians had no say) gave three counties of Bessarabia east of the River Prut on Moldavia's eastern side to Russia.

In 1856 the Congress of Paris, ending the Crimean War, re-assigned them to Moldavia. It also allowed the elections in Moldavia and Wallachia which led in 1859 to the union of the two principalities – though still under Turkish suzerainty. This "union" is remembered in many Romanian street names. In 1940, when Romania was effectively under Nazi control, the USSR delivered an ultimatum demanding the return of the Bessarabian territory and the cession in addition of the northern half of Moldavia's Bucovina region. In 1944, when Romania turned to fight the Axis powers which had formerly controlled it, Stalin invaded these regions. They are still in the USSR.

The Romanians naturally aren't pleased. Outside their country a separate Soviet Republic of Moldavia has been established, using a language which Stalin defined as "Moldavian". Romanians say that it's ordinary Romanian, and support the Soviet Moldavians' demand for unification with themselves.

No principality of Moldavia exists today. But it still forms a conveniently clear geographical unit. Its eastern frontier lies along the River Prut, its western on the Carpathian peaks. Southward, it stretches to the beginnings of the Danube Plain. To the north it's still marked by the extraordinary 10 m-high wire fence, punctuated with frequent guard towers, which the Russians erected between themselves and their Warsaw Pact allies. Don't let this fence give you picture-scoop ideas. Photographing frontier areas is still illegal in Romania. The Russians guards won't like it, either – and they have guns.

As far as this chapter is concerned, then, Moldavia means four pairs of modern counties, one mountain, one rolling plateau, arranged side by side as you travel north – Vrancea, Galati (or part of it); Bacau, Vaslui; Neamt, Iasi; and Suceava, Botosani.

The Southern Approaches

If you set out northward to Moldavia from Bucharest, the first part of the journey's dull. By road you take the DN2 to Urziceni, as you did on your way to Constanta, and continue on it to Buzau, Rimnicu Sarat, and Focsani, 177 km altogether. Up to Focsani almost the only point of interest is the fact that from Buzau on (110 km from Bucharest) you have the Carpathian foothills rising direct from the plain on your left.

The train route starts by going due north to the oil town of Ploiesti in the Carpathian foothills, 60 km from Bucharest, and then turns northeast, following the Carpathians' curving edge. From Buzau on it stays within sight of the DN2 as far as Roman.

If you come from Tulcea (your base for exploring the Danube Delta – Chapter Five) you have to cross the Danube. You can do this by following the DN22 from Tulcea to Braila (74 km). This gives you a chance to see the 18th century mosque at Macin and to visit the recently-discovered underground 4th century church at Niculitel, just off the road (Chapter Five). From Macin you can take a short cut direct to Galati by a side road.

The Danube crossings at Galati and Braila have to be made on ferries. These are simple flat pontoons that you can drive straight onto, and they're free unless you arrive before or after regular operating hours (roughly 06.00-22.00), when you pay for a "special" crossing. The fee's little more than the £2–£3 you'd expect to pay anyway for a similar crossing in Britain.

If you're without a car you can also sail between Tulcea and Galati, and on to Braila, by boat or hovercraft. If you do this you'll find it a fascinating – and relaxing – way of travelling through a lush green countryside, with Russia on one bank and Romania on the other nearly all the way.

Braila and Galati are both ancient settlements, and both Danube ports, now losing their importance because of ships' increasing size and the Danube Canal's short cut. Larger vessels find docking at Constanta easier, and the Danube Canal saves smaller vessels bound for inland upstream ports a lot of time and trouble. At first sight neither town's specially attractive, though both have spots worth seeing.

Both places suffered severely through being for years on the frontier between Turkey and Romania. The Turks dominated Braila from 1544 to 1829, though it was constantly fought over and frequently changed hands. The Romanians took possession for good in 1829, but only after the town had been almost totally destroyed by fire. It was rebuilt around the harbour area on a semi-circular grid plan in 1831–35.

Grain stores overlooking the quayside date from 1888–89. They were built by Anghel Saligny, famous mainly for his Cernavoda bridge (Chapter Five). They're said to contain the world's earliest prefabricated concrete panels. The town's main Orthodox church is a former 17th century mosque, converted in 1829, after the Turks' withdrawal. There's also a Greek church, whose building began in 1862. Remains of the once-important Turkish fort still exist.

Galati lies 32 km from Braila by DN2B. Like Braila it was a major medieval harbour and market town. When the Turks swept northward it was the only seaport to remain under Romanian control. In 1944 however, when Romania's revolt forced a Nazi withdrawal, the Germans blew up the harbour, shipyards, factories, warehouses, and several thousand dwellings. Despite that, a number of old churches and other fine buildings still exist. They include the 16th century Precista fortified church, and the Vovidenia and Mavromol churches, as well as the State Theatre.

Galati offers three good hotels, two of them in the town's main B-dul Republicii. Most of what you might want to see lies in or near this thoroughfare. There's a good campsite on a turning off the DN26 about 15 km north of the town.

If you're driving to northern Moldavia you'll need to leave Galati county and cut across from Braila or Galati to the DN2 in the region of Focsani, Vrancea county's capital. Like the two Danube towns Focsani isn't at first sight exciting. However, its main post office, still in use at 81 Strada Mare a Unirii, is famous for having served up to 1859 as the Moldavia–Wallachia frontier post. An inscription on the building's side records that the removal of the frontier here was the first move towards Romania's unification. Hence the street's name – Main Street of Unity.

Southern Moldavia

The Vrancea region, home of shepherds and foresters from ancient times, is renowned for its handicrafts and folklore. In particular, it's famous as the home of the Miorita (Little Lamb) ballad. For visitors however Focsani is just another undistinguished lowland town. One of Romania's many medieval citadel-fortresses lies at its western edge. Odobesti, 8 km northwest, is the centre of one of Moldavia's best-known wine-growing areas. Cellars dating from 1839 have been restored for modern use. But long before they were built Odobesti's wines were popular with the Polish aristocracy and Cossack merchants, as well as Moldavia's princes.

If you're travelling north by train or driving on the main DN2 from Bucharest you'll find that the scenery changes somewhat around Focsani. You still have the Carpathians to the west swinging gently upward from level land. But there are now continuous stretches of low hills to the east in place of the seemingly endless flat plain further south.

You're in the valley of the River Siret, which rises beyond Romania's present northern border with the USSR. For centuries merchants used it to carry their wares upstream as well as down. Today it's being dammed at a number of places to provide electricity in fairly small quantities and water for controlled irrigation. The meandering Prut flows roughly parallel with the Siret at a distance of 40–100 km east and marks the frontier with Russia all the way from the Danube a few kilometres east of Galati to Moldavia's furthest point north.

Marasesti is almost the only place of interest in this southern section of your route. Or perhaps I'd better say that you'll not be able to face your Romanian friends unless you can say you've seen the mausoleum at Marasesti. It's a memorial to Romanian soldiers killed in the battle for the town in 1917, when German and Austro–Hungarian forces launched a major offensive from the north. Hardly anyone in Britain has any idea, even, that WWI's fighting extended to Romania. Nevertheless, the Romanians won a decisive victory here which finally prevented Moldavia being detached from Wallachia. For them the battle still represents a decisive step towards final unity.

A year previously attacks had been launched from Transylavania, then of course part of Austria–Hungary, across the Carpathians, and also from

Turnu–Severin (Chapter Eleven) into the Danube Plain. The southern attack had succeeded. Bucharest had been occupied, and the Romanian Government had been compelled to move to Iasi in Moldavia (below).

The 1916 offensive through Transylvania had depended on the Germans forcing their way over various passes through the Carpathians. One was the Oituz carrying the road that links Brasov (Chapter Nine) to the Siret valley (where we now are), which the Romanians had also successfully defended. Apart from any historical interest however this is one of the Carpathians' outstandingly beautiful regions. You can reach it by forking northwest at Adjud, about 20 km north of Marasesti.

Barely 40 km on you reach Onesti, known for forty years as Gheorghe Gheorghiu-Dej after the Communist leader (Chapter Twelve). It's modern, with foul factories. It was formed from two villages. In one of them, Borzesti, Stephen the Great, Moldavia's outstanding 15th century ruler (Chapter Twelve), is believed to have been born. He and his son Alexandru certainly built a small church here in 1493. Its design is notable for its early combination of the older three-apse plan with a lengthened nave (as we Westerners would call it) and the decorations on its outside walls. The grim chemical factory opposite is notable for its pollutants and its smell.

The town stands at the foot of two routes over the Carpathians, the main Oituz road and one following the more northerly Trotus valley (Chapter Nine) past the little town of Tirgu Ocna. This little spot was once famous for the salt mined there and floated down the Tazlau river to Bacau and the Siret. Its sodium chloride goes now to Onesti's factories.

From Onesti, where there's a hotel with reasonably good ratings, you can make a short southward car excursion to Casin, to see one of Romania's innumerable remarkable small all-wooden churches, and to Manastirea Casin (Casin Monastery), whose church dates from 1655 and was once well fortified. You can also visit Tirgu Ocna, mentioned above, and another fortress-monastery, Raducanu, and go by a side road from Tirgu Ocna to the little mountain spa of Slanic Moldova. For car tourists campsites near the spa make a good sightseeing base.

You can return to the DN2 at Bacau, 60 km north of Adjud, by taking the DN11's northward arm from Gheorghe Gheorghiu-Dej. Bacau has been a vital communications centre for centuries. It isn't a very alluring town today. It has three decently-equipped modern hotels, but its only tourist attraction is the Precista church in Strada 9 Mai, built by Stephen the Great's son Alexandru. It was orginally attached to the palace Stephen (Chapter Twelve) built for his son, whom he put in charge of Southern Moldavia while he campaigned elsewhere.

The main Bucharest–Suceava railway line continues steadily northward up the Siret valley to Roman and Pascani, where it switches to the River Suceava's valley. The road keeps closer to the Carpathian foothills, with open land sloping gently to the Siret and the rolling hills of Moldavia's lower area to its east.

Piatra Neamt, Bicaz, and the Ceahlau Massif

If you want to see another of Moldavia's extraordinarily attractive regions turn northwest at Bacau onto the DN15 for the 60 km to Piatra Neamt (Neamt's county town) or take the train there. Some Suceava expresses include through coaches to Piatra, as the locals call it, that are detached at Bacau.

Your route from Bacau takes you up the long, fertile, very beautiful valley of the River Bistrita, which rises high on the Prislop Pass separating Moldavia from the Maramures (Chapter Seven). Like the Siret's, its waters were used as a transport route in the days when railways didn't exist and roads were at best merely muddy tracks. Gold was panned, too, in its upper reaches. And today it feeds the huge artificial Lake Bicaz, built to supply electricity to a wide area, in a superbly scenic valley high above Piatra Neamt on lonely Deahlau Massif's eastern, Moldavian side.

If you arrive at Piatra Neamt station, close to the Bistrita river, with the bus station almost opposite, walk directly away from it, northward, up B-dul Republicii, passing the Bulevard and Central, two of Piatra's three modern hotels. This takes you into Strada Karl Marx, which runs roughly east-west at the foot of the old town's central area. You come almost face to face with an imposing statue of Stephen the Great. The Ceahlau Hotel, the town's best, lies a little up to your right.

You can reach the Sfintu Ioan (St John) church and its 19 m-high lookout steeple, both built before 1500, during Stephen the Great's reign, by taking the turning to your left on Karl Marx Street's further side. Just below the church (you're climbing all the time) you pass the County Historical Museum (Muzeul judetean de istorie), such as every Romanian county town possesses. This one has quite a good collection, and is also

labelled Muzeu Arheologicu. A little beyond the church you'll find the underground remains of the palace (the Romanians, as usual, call it "princely court") built in the 15th century. They lie below a grammar school named after Petru Rares, another of Moldavia's outstanding Princes, who ruled in the first half of the 16th century.

Piatra's surrounded by hills going up to 690 m. On one of them, Bitca Doamnei, the remains of a Dacian fortress have been discovered. Cozla Hill above St John's church has been turned into a fine natural park, with a number of restaurants in it. There are other parks in the town and plentiful flowers are a cheering feature of its old centre (the dull tall blocks of flats around the outskirts aren't as eye-catching). Several old buildings are worth hunting out, including a wooden house at 23 Strada Alexandru cel Bun and the former manor house at 191 Strada Stefan cel Mare, now a hospital, near the "princely court".

Piatra's surrounding scenery is magnificent, as you'll have discovered on your way from Bacau. If you continue up the DN15 towards Bicaz you can turn off right after 6 km to the fine monastery of Bistrita, built in 1407 by Alexander the Good (Chapter Twelve) to be his family's burial place. He himself, his first wife, and Alexandru, Stephen the Great's son, are all buried here, as are the later princes and leaders. A museum housed in the tower which Stephen himself added to the church displays among its collection two icons presented to Alexander the Good by the Byzantine Paleolog Emperor Johannes VIII. Families descended from the Byzantine Paleologs, carrying the surname Paleolog, still live in Romania.

41

In the lovely, forested hills above Bistrita you'll find another ancient monastery, Bisericani, built in 1512. Your chief destination along the main road however will probably be Bicaz, 28 km from Piatra. It's a modern settlement in a magnificent mountain setting, dependent on the hydro-electric station at the 35 km-long storage lake's southern tip. It's also a major tourist centre, with a small hotel, a motel, chalets, and campsite. You can make boat trips on the lake, drive round most of it and onto the Ceahlau, one of Romania's major Nature Reserves, and walk through superb mountain scenery on a number of marked paths, both on Ceahlau itself and in other directions. The upper parts of Ceahlau show the Carpathians at their rockiest and most awesome, very different from the friendlier lower forested slopes. Lots of coach excursions come through Bicaz. You can join one for a more sedentary view of the region.

Mount Ceahlau covers an area of 300 sq km and rises to a height of 1904 m, with several peaks little below that level. The famous Romanian writer, Alexandru Vlahuta, who spent a lot of time in this region, described it as "the old king of the Moldavian Carpathians". It stands out bold and clear from many regions in Transylvania as well as Moldavia. Much of its scenery includes cliffs and precipices up to 150 m high, and many species of protected trees and plants grow on its slopes. For that reason the entire massif is a Nature Reserve.

Many Ceahlau species have still not been properly studied. But any walker on its sometimes stony, sometimes grassy tracks will notice levels of beech forest between 400 and 700 m, with mixed firs and beeches at the higher levels. The spruce level from 1000 up is preceded by mixed firs and spruce and followed by a stratum of dwarf pine, juniper, and bilberry. Magnificent larches grow at various points, with a special reservation at a spot called Criminis. Botanists can find an enormous range of shrubs, flowers, and lichens here. The DN12C from Bicaz takes you southwest into Transylvania (Chapter Nine).

Agapia

Despite all this superb scenery the biggest tourist attraction in Piatra Neamt's catchment area is probably Agapia Monastery. It lies about 40 km north of Piatra. You take the DN15C from there towards Tirgu Neamt and turn off westward about 7 km short of the town. The turning's clearly signposted for "Manastirea Agapia".

Buses operate to Agapia villlage, about 1 km short of the monastery, from the bus station (*Autogara*) beside Piatra Neamt's railway station. But they're not frequent. If you're energetic you can catch one of the much more frequent buses to Tirgu Neamt (make certain it goes via Baltatesti, on the 15C, not via Razboieni: departure times and routes are clearly listed at the bus station's ticket windows). You have to get off at the Agapia turning (*intersectie spre Agapia*), so make this clear to the driver.

From the main road you've a 7 km (4¼ mile) walk to the monastery. gently uphill all the way. But if you look foreign (which you can't help doing) and have the sense to carry your gear in a back pack (as sensible travellers in wilder places always do) the locals are unlikely to let you walk the whole way. A few months after the Christmas 1989 revolution in Romania, hearing that the monasteries were having a hard time through food shortages and other problems, I decided I simply must pay my Agapia friends a visit.

I hadn't walked far up this road before a cheery peasant woman in a bright red patterned skirt, driving an enormously long cart pulled by a pretty cantankerous horse, slowed down and signalled me to throw my pack aboard and jump up beside her. When she stopped to go into the village shop I walked on, but was flagged down almost immediately by a nun driving a smart Dacia 1300 station waggon. She turned out to be the Mother Superior's secretary, and I was deposited in style at the monastery's main door.

Agapia's position is lovely. It stands 450 m above sea level, right in the mouth of a steep-sided, heavily-forested narrow valley that begins where the Eastern Carpathians rise from gently-inclined land. Founded in 1447, its buildings were burned by Turks in 1821 and rebuilt in 1823. Nicolae Grigorescu, Romania's best-loved painter, began copying icons there as a boy and later painted all the figures on the main church's silver-clad iconostasis. Thousands of tourists of all nationalities flock to Agapia in summer to see the church, soak in the monastery's magnificent setting, and enjoy its excellent museum. It displays all sorts of carpets and embroidery produced by the monastery's own nuns in past centuries, as well as gifts presented to its abbesses by visiting potentates, such as one of Russia's czars.

The monastery's built in square fortress shape, with its main church standing in the middle of a quadrangle of two-storeyed buildings that have sheltering balconies at both levels. The church isn't at all large by our standards. There's a vestibule (*pronaos* , to be technical) where you

can buy picture postcards (scarce in Romania) and illustrated books about Agapia in various languages. The body of the church is covered by carpets and totally uncluttered by seats, though there are some attached to the walls. Icons stand at various points. But the main thing you'll notice is the magnificent silver-framed iconostasis with its paintings of biblical characters and saints and the hanging lamps burning constantly in front of it.

A fairly large village of small wooden houses of traditional Moldavian design surrounds the monastery's main building on three sides. They belong to senior nuns, who have no money of their own but whose families are allowed to build or buy dwellings for them. With its four hundred nuns Agapia today is Romania's largest monastery. Despite a law dating from 1960 which makes it illegal for anyone under 30 to join a monastery numbers have increased steadily from 1968's three hundred, and a large proportion today are young indeed.

On a casual visit to Agapia you won't see many of these ladies except perhaps in church during the Sunday liturgy which starts at about 08.30 and goes on till after 11.00. But they lead extremely busy lives.

They're up at 05.30 every day, when the first service of the day begins with some remarkably fine singing even when the church is freezing cold (Orthodox services are designed to be sung, not said). By 07.00 or so they're off to breakfast and their various jobs – working in the busy kitchen, cleaning the place, working on the stunning church embroideries they produce for the entire Iasi Metropolitanate (bishopric, roughly speaking), weaving superb carpets from wool produced by their own sheep, setting up and working on the knitting machines which produce garments not only for themselves but also for needy families nearby, cutting out and sewing fabric garments similarly used, painting icons, attending choir rehearsals, sewing the amazingly decorated shrouds in which monks and nuns are wrapped before burial, going off to classes maybe in modern languages (to cope with the monastery's summer flock of visitors), maybe in history, or cooking, or farmwork. Educational needs sometimes even take the nuns to countries like Switzerland or Britain. The Orthodox churches have their own travel network.

The monastery owns about 400 ha of land on which they raise their own cattle, sheep, pigs, and chickens, as well as vegetables (on a high hillside 7 km up the valley) and fruit (there's a fine orchard). They have extensive hothouses, where flowers, fruit, and vegetables are grown all year round. There are byres and sheds where the animals spend much of the year: spring comes late and winter early at altitudes such as Agapia's.

The monastery also has its own builders' yard, supplied largely by timber from its own woodlands. A number of men are allowed to help with the heavy work, but you're quite likely to see the Mother Superior herself standing in the middle of the yard giving directions.

Despite all this practical work the nuns take their spiritual life very seriously indeed. At one point in Holy Week (leading up to Easter, a time of spiritual preparation) the Mother Superior has to spend eighteen continuous hours in the church – while still managing all the monastery's innumerable activities and attending innumerable other services.

On top of all that she also maintains accommodation for a fair number of special guests, who are treated like lords. The nuns not only grow their own meat, eggs, and vegetables. They also make their own butter, bake their own bread, and produce a fine cheese from a mixture of cows' and ewes' milk. They're proud of their cuisine. Good coversation – in French or Romanian – is also a tradition at the Mother Superior's capacious and ever-hospitable table. Innumerable well-known writers and intellectuals have been enjoying it for decades.

On a recent visit I found the difference between Agapia and Romania's towns very striking. The towns were run down, and their atmosphere often worried and edgy. Essentials could sometimes be in short supply. Agapia on the other hand was very spick and span in every respect. The nuns seemed to have everything they needed. And everyone, including the countryfolk living round about, was obviously happy.

Unfortunately, the monastery itself can't keep open house for all comers. For Romanians a standard form of holiday is to hire a room for a week or two in one of the nuns' houses – not only at Agapia but also at many other magnificiently-located monasteries. At Agapia however everyone can find accommodation and meals in the pleasant small hotel ("inn") in Agapia village, a kilometre or so below the monastery. It becomes crowded in high summer, though.

Around Agapia

Agapia – village or monastery – makes an excellent base for walking in the high surrounding hills, and also for combining this with a modicum of car excursions.

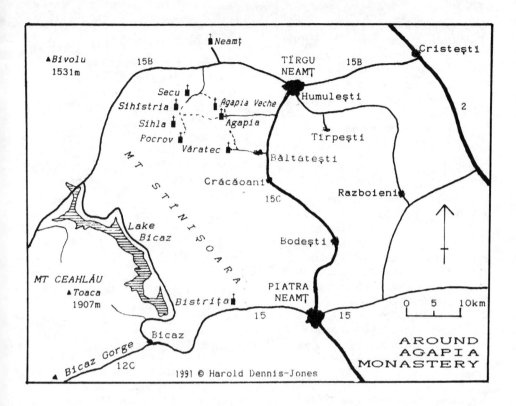

On the map:

Neamţ
Bivolu 1531m
15B
TÏRGU NEAMŢ
15B
Cristeşti
Secu
Sihīstria
Agapia Veche
Humuleşti
2
Sihla
Agapia
Pocrov
Văratec
Tîrpeşti
MT STÎNIŞOARA
Băltăteşti
Crácăoani
15C
Razboieni
Lake Bicaz
Bodeşti
MT CEAHLĂU
Toaca 1907m
Bistriţa
PIATRA NEAMŢ
0 5 10km
Bicaz
15
15
Bicaz Gorge
12C
AROUND AGAPIA MONASTERY
1991 © Harold Dennis-Jones

On the main approach road, a little before you reach the monastery's chief entrance, you'll see separate signs pointing to Manastirea Varatec in one direction, and to Agapia Veche (Old Agapia) in the other. A third route goes to the monastery's left (south of it) and straight on up the valley behind it.

You can drive to Varatec, which lies about 7 km to the south. There's also a direct turning to it from the main Piatra–Tirgu Neamt road (DN15C), parallel with the one to Agapia further north. Alternatively you can walk to it from Agapia over the hills by a more or less motorable track through magnificently-forested landscapes. A picnic area with lovely views makes a pleasant stopping-place on this route. But even in summer don't rely on being able to buy soft drinks or anything else on the spot. Get what you need in Agapia village.

Varatec dates from 1785, though built on the site of a 1598 hermitage. Like Agapia, it has a notable museum. Like Agapia, too, it has played host to many writers who have come for relaxation in its magnificent setting. One of them, the poetess Veronica Micle, is buried at Varatec. Its buildings are far fewer however and its size far smaller than Agapia's.

The route to Agapia Veche starts as a very rough road between single-storey houses and past a well. You have the monastery's private cemetery on a steep knoll to your left. It's a wonderfully peaceful spot, with pleasant views, well worth a half-hour's exploration. The road becomes a footpath when you have to leave a

45

broad private forestry road and take a steep track to your right. It's marked with a blue cross on a white square. Though it's a very grassy track, passing through a forest made up mainly of immensely tall Sitka spruces, it's still rough enough to make walking boots or trainers advisable – outside hot, dry summer days at least.

The path passes a former hermit's dwelling and after about twenty minutes brings you to Agapia Veche, a little mountain monastery in a hillside forest clearing. It's surrounded by a fence high enough to keep out wolves and bears and other unwelcome intruders. But you'll be welcome to go in and see its tiny church and other, mainly wooden, buildings. Agapia Veche, originally known as Agapia din Deal (Agapia on the Hill) is probably a little older than Agapia din Vale (Agapia in the Valley), which we call simply Agapia.

The main path, marked by a blue bar across a white rectangle, which started at Varatec, goes to Agapia Veche's right and continues – a good two hours' walking in all – to Secu Monastery, yet another valley-guarding monastery, built in stone in the mid-16th century. It has for centuries been a place of learning, and has seen its share of warfare. The Polish King Jan Sobieski billeted his troops here in 1691, and the last engagement against Turkish troops took place near the monastery in 1821.

The monastery's main buildings were carefully restored some twenty years ago. Its museum contains precious embroideries, silverware, and old books. But many of its best pieces are on display – or soon will be again – in Romania's national Art Gallery, housed in Bucharest's former Royal Palace and badly damaged during the 1989 revolution.

When you come down out of the forest to Secu you cross a small stream and turn left along an unsurfaced road. If you follow this road you'll come to yet another monastery, Sihistria. It lies at the end of the motorable track and is home to a number of monks. On red letter holy days, such as the Feast of All Saints, local people pour out in all weathers to Sihistria. I've known the church full enough to rival Bucharest's Metro: there was hardly room to squeeze another body in.

If you're driving to Secu and Sihistria go first to Tirgu Neamt, turn west onto the DN15B, then turn south onto a rough side road. You travel to Sihistria on this track. The DN 15B continues as an alternative route to Bicaz.

Beyond Sihistria you can walk up into the forests, making for yet another monastery, called Sihla. There may still be a few signposts among the trees. But don't take them too literally. On this path, in the course of a few hours' walking, we once passed three successive signs which all said: Manastirea Sihla cinci kilometri – Sihla Monastery five kilometres. You need to know that in Romanian *cinci* (five) is simply *the* indefinite number. It doesn't mean five. It means something more than one but less than, say, twelve or twenty, "Five minutes" is used in much the same way. If anyone asks how long anything takes you always reply: "Cinci minuti" (pronounced roughly *chinch minOOT*).

From Sihla you can turn and come back to Agapia – assuming you've left someone to drive the car back from Sihistria – by the path down the valley leading directly to the monastery. But if you're thinking of making the circuit of these monasteries in a long day's walking I'd recommend starting up the valley beyond the monastery and returning via Sihistria and Secu. The signposting is somewhat better. If you like it's possible also to visit yet another tiny forest-clearing monastery, Schitul Pocrov or Procov, south of Sihla.

Best of all, of course, spend several days exploring the whole area. Mountains and forests, composed mainly of enormous pines but with a plentiful variety of trees interspersed, are magnificent. You've a chance of seeing all sorts of wildlife – though wolf and bear appear only in really cold winters.

Manastirea Neamt

There's one more monastery you ought to know about before you leave this region – Neamt. It lies to the north off the DN15B road going west out of Tirgu Neamt a little past the turning to Secu. Like Secu and Agapia it still retains its fortress-like layout and, as at other monasteries, the outline of earlier structures revealed by excavations are traced on the grass beside its church.

Because of its importance, Neamt Monastery is clearly signposted. It's believed to be the oldest of all Moldavia's monasteries. It was in being before the end of 13th century. Additions were made by Alexander the Good (Chapter Twelve), and the present majestic church was built by Stephen the Great in 1497, after his defeat of King John Albert of Poland (Chapter Twelve). It was the first Moldavian-style church, with three apses and a long nave, to have an enclosed porch, and its interior murals are very striking. Stephen the Great is depicted in some of them.

For centuries Neamt has been a centre of learning and art. A magnificent shroud, embroidered at Neamt in 1437, is now the property of Bucharest's National Gallery of Art. The monastery's library contains a large number of valuable incunabula and medieval manuscripts. Today the monastery houses the Metropolitanate of Iasi's busy printing works.

Don't believe the asses who tell you bibles are scarce in Romania; the Patriarchate has a central Bible Press and the Metropolitanates all have their own additional presses. Hospitable Romanians can't bring themselves to refuse bibles thrust on them by well-meaning "missionaries" (mostly American). But they find acceptance decidedly distasteful.

You have to drive through Tirgu Neamt from Agapia to reach Manastirea Neamt. As its name implies – Tirgu is a Slav-derived word meaning "market" – it was once a thriving international medieval market town, with one of Romania's many medieval citadels on a hill above the town, half-an-hour's walk from the centre. But it was overtaken in importance by Piatra Neamt and it's pretty dull today.

The bus station's tucked away in messy, anonymous central side streets and the railway station, brand new in 1987, is hidden towards the town's eastern edge, with only one tiny sign in the town's centre telling you which way to set out, and a still-unsurfaced stretch of road taking you the last few hundred metres to it. If you ask anyone the way they'll say simply: "Straight on". If your way-finding ability's as poor as mine allow an hour or two for getting to the station – or take a taxi (if you can find one).

Once you've got there it may be worth

noting that there are a couple of through trains every day to Bucharest. They link up with main line expresses at Pascani, due east of Tirgu Neamt. You reserve a seat when you buy your ticket, and because the trains are never full when they start you can reckon on a reasonably comfortable journey much of the way to Bucharest.

If you're prepared to walk from the town centre you can get up to the ruins of Neamt Citadel (Cetatea) in half an hour. These citadels served much the same function as our medieval castles, but seem never to have been regular residences. There are good views from this one.

If you've a car, or are game for a longer walk, try one other excursion from Tirgu Neamt. It's to the little village of Tirpesti, about 12 km southwest. Tirpesti's part of Petriceni commune, and off the bus route through Razboieni (above). These are the names you'll see on the early signposts, though you can orient the start of your journey by going past the little museum house that commemorates the Romanian writer Ion Creanga in the suburb of Humulesti. That's clearly signposted. After 7 or 8 km you have to fork right onto a side turning and ford a fairly wide but shallow stream. Another 3 km or so brings you to Tirpesti.

The village's interest lies in the extraordinary little museum assembled there mainly through the efforts of an ordinary local man, Nicolae Popa. He has collected all sort of things belonging to the village and the area around it. They include magnificent old traditional costumes worth enormous sums today, prehistoric pottery, superbly grotesque masks still used in traditional village festivities, old farm implements, Roman coins, and

even some British coins from the 1920s. Popa himself, a considerable though wholly self-taught artist, has sold sculptures to several Romanian galleries.

Suceava and the "Painted Churches"

Your easiest way of reaching Suceava from Agapia or Tirgu Neamt is to take the DN15B eastward from Tirgu Neamt to its junction with the DN2 just south of Cristesti, and then turn north. As a little diversion, you may like to take a side-road leading east after about 15 km to Forasti and Tatarusi. If you turn north at this second village you'll come to the monastery of Probota. Its church's outside walls are almost as magnificently decorated as the Three Hierarchs in Iasi (below). You can continue past Probota and turn west to rejoin the DN2. Alternatively, about 25 km after you join the DN2 from Tirgu Neamt, a side turning on your left, beyond Fundu Moldovei, takes you to the fine 16th century fortress-style Risca Monastery.

Back on the DN2 (or still on it) you'll find the road now leaves the Carpathian's edge and heads north across rolling open land. Beyond Falticeni it becomes marshy. With luck you may see a whole series of storks standing quietly fishing beside pools and streams.

Rail travel from Tirgu Neamt to Suceava involves changing at Pascani. Trains aren't frequent.

Suceava itself, built on the river of the same name, is the capital of the Bucovina, Moldavia's most northerly section. But it was also Moldavia's capital for two centuries up to 1565. It prospered most in Stephen the Great's time, when it acted as a centre of overland trade and as Moldavia's main customs post. Large warehouses have survived from that period. The town's approaches are cluttered with blocks of flats up to ten storeys high, but the central area on higher land to the north contains much of interest. It's the town's oldest part, though now rather altered, and has a 19th century area south of it, with a pleasant park in its centre. The ruins of three ancient citadel-castles stand on hills in the town's east, west, and northwest.

The huge Old Princely Citadel to the east, built largely by Stephen the Great, has been thoroughly excavated. It's a very impressive structure, with an enormous moat and vast walls. You get a good view over the town from here. The later Zamca Citadel, reached via Strada Zamca, was transformed into a strong fortress by the invading King Jan Sobieski of Poland in 1691. Its views to the mountains and into the Suceava valley are superb. The Scheia Citadel in the town's northwest dates from the 14th century. It's considered Moldavia's oldest stone-built citadel. But only a few walls remain.

The town contains several fine old churches. The 14th century Mirauti in Strada Mirautilor is the oldest, followed by the Sfintu Gheorghe Nou (New St George) in Aleea Ion Voda Viteazul (1514), the Sfintu Dumitru in Strada Stefan cel Mare (1535), the Invierii on the corner of Ana Ipatescu and Iona Voda (1552), and the Ioan Botezatorul in Stefanita Voda (1643). For good measure there's also an Armenian church built by an Armenian merchant in 1512 at the end of Strada Armeneasca.

The Mirauti is specially notable because of its enamelled roof tiles. The St George has fine interior frescos and remains of some external 16th century murals.

Suceava possesses four good hotels (though they're often occupied largely by coach parties in summer). One of them, the Suceava in Strada N. Balcvescu, conveniently has Tarom's offices on one side of it and the Tourist Office and the railway "agentie" on the other.

For most tourists, who may have flown into Suceava from Bucharest or the coast, the town's the kicking-off point for a coach tour of the Bucovina's five remarkable "Painted Churches", so-called because their exterior as well as interior walls are covered with stupendous 16th century frescos. In over 400 years the colours of most have never even dimmed. At least two used paints whose chemical composition has never been unravelled. Quite apart from their artistic value the paintings are notable historical and social documents. Not surprisingly, UNESCO includes them on its world heritage list.

As if all that weren't enough the churches are set in outstandingly beautiful mountain scenery, among soaring green hills and mighty forests. Two of them – Moldovita and Sucevita – belong to fortress-monasteries whose fortifications still exist in carefully-restored form. Taking a one-day coach tour round them is, in a way, a bit of an insult. You can't possibly even begin to appreciate either the paintings' details and skill or the churches' architecture and their stunning settings until you've spent much more time with them. Perhaps the answer is a quick first look, and more later visits – several of them.

With your own car you can see the churches at leisure. One possible circuit is to leave Suceava by the good old DN2, heading this time towards

Siret and the USSR frontier (good view of the friendly tall frontier fence). Turn off left at Slobozia Suceavei towards Radauti and left again 6 km later at Milisauti. Another 11 km brings you to Arbore.

It's the smallest of the "Painted Churches", with no cupola on its roof because its founder was merely a minor landowner (a boyar), not an aristocrat. If you really understand Moldavian church architecture you can tell the founder/builder's precise rank from the towers and cupolas on its roof.

Arbore is famous for the delicacy and liveliness of its paintings, and for their use of five different shades of green. The church's courtyard still preserves the heavy stone slabs in which fifteen recesses served for paint-mixing.

Retrace your route to Milisauti, and continue to Radauti, where you turn southwest towards Cimpulung Moldovenesc on the DN17A. You reach Sucevita village after 21 km, with the monastery just outside it. Sucevita is quite simply breathtaking, particularly if you take the trouble to walk up the hillside to the south and look into the fortified courtyard from there.

The church's frescos are breathtaking, too. The walls seem to be covered with thousands of portraits. The southern wall carries a superb Tree of Jesse, a pictorial genealogy demonstrating the connection between Old and New Testaments. There's a frieze of the scholars and philosophers of antiquity. Pythagoras, Sophocles, Plato, Aristotle, and Solon are all gorgeously arrayed in Byzantine cloaks. The "Virgin's Prayer" shows endless scenes of horses, citadels, and people in oriental dress. The Virgin Mary herself is depicted as a Byzantine Empress under a large red veil held by angels. The outside of the apse shows all the world's hierarchies – seraphs, angels, prophets, apostles, bishops, martyrs. Their sober colours are heightened by the red of their clothes and the gold of their haloes. But that's only a beginning.

From Sucevita continue another 30 km to Vatra Moldovitei village, with Moldovita Monastery just north of it. The church was built in 1532 and painted in 1537. Here again, there are hundreds of separate scenes. Here, Jesse's Tree is shown against a dark blue background, and one of the most interesting compositions depicts the siege of Constantinople. The town had fallen to the Turks eighty years previously. But hatred of everything Turkish was very strong. Moldovita's fortifications are less impressive than Sucevita's. But the surrounding scenery is just as magnificent.

There are small hotels and campsites close to both Moldovita and Sucevita. Buses pass close, and a railway branch line ends at Moldovita.

From there turn southeast for the 14 km run to join the DN17 at Vama (its name shows it was an old frontier customs post). After another 16 km a short turning on your right takes you to Voronet. The church here stands almost alone. The buildings that once surrounded it have been destroyed, but its frescos are as magnificent as ever, except on the northern wall where they've been damaged by bad weather. They're famous for the blue they use – Jesse's Tree here develops in an explosion of blue – and for a dramatic Last Judgement. The fire of Gehenna is shown as a giant funnel of live coals flaming at Jesus' feet, and the sinners destined for incineration include famous people, such as heretic kings and schismatic popes.

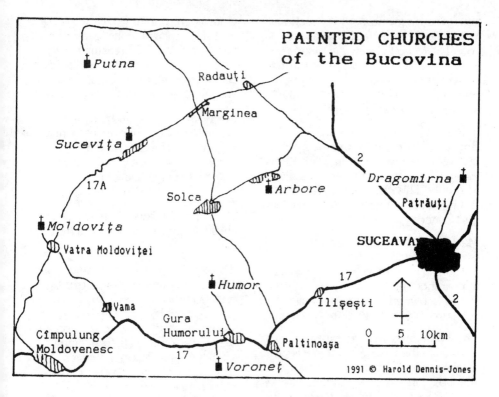

PAINTED CHURCHES of the Bucovina

Putna
Radauți
Marginea
Sucevița
17A
Solca
Arbore
2
Dragomirna
Patrăuți
Moldovița
Vatra Moldoviței
SUCEAVA
Humor
17
Ilișești
2
Vama
Gura Humorului
Cîmpulung Moldovenesc
17
Paltinoașa
Voroneț
0   5   10km
1991 © Harold Dennis-Jones

Elsewhere, sinners are dressed as Turks and Tatars. In the Resurrection of the Dead the Last Trump is depicted as a bucium – a traditional Romanian instrument resembling an alphorn. But this is only a tiny part of what you can enjoy at Voronet.

Humor, which you reach by going back to the main DN17, turning right and then going left almost immediately from Gura Humorului, has had some of its outside paintings damaged by weather. But a lovely Return of the Prodigal Son still remains, and the church's situation, 6 km up a beautiful valley, with the entrance tower and parts of the surrounding walls still surviving, is enchanting.

For me Humor is specially memorable because of an incredible *Heilige Nacht* I recorded there many years ago. Heilige Nacht was composed in 1819 while the Bucovina was ruled by the Austrians. We know that the carol spread so fast among countryfolk, who were then mostly illiterate, that it was thought to be a folksong. In Moldavia the Romanians had reshaped it from its original 3/4 time into their own predominant 2/2 rhythm, and the choir I recorded, led by the priest's wife, sang it with astonishing harmonies all their own. I could hardly believe my ears when I realised what was going onto my tape.

It's 48 km in all from Humor back to Suceava. On the way you pass a campsite at Ilisesti, 19 km from the town, which provides another possible touring base.

The Rest of the Bucovina

The "Painted Churches" and the stupendous scenery they're set in

51

aren't the Bucovina's only attractions. Following the route outlined above you can stop off in Patrauti, 9 km from Suceava, and make a 4 km detour to see yet another church founded by Stephen the Great – one that's tiny and modest. It dates from 1487.

In Radauti, 37 km from Suceava, the Bogdana Church gets it name from the fact that it was built in 1359–65 by Bodgan I, the earliest ruler of medieval Moldavia. This church, too, is modest. But it holds the tombs of Moldavia's first Princes.

Marginea, 8 km along the road to Sucevita, has for centuries been producing pottery given a totally black appearance through incomplete firing. A well-known modern potter still carries on the old tradition.

From Marginea you can turn north and rejoin the road you left in Radauti. It takes you to Putna, in many ways the most famous of all the monasteries still in Romania that were founded by Stephen the Great. The road runs close to low hills that form the frontier with the USSR. Many more of Stephen the Great's churches and monasteries lie beyond the border. But Stephen himself is buried at Putna.

The monastery was built by him in 1466–69 and destroyed and restored several times since then. The massive church still stands. But of the original fortifications only the entrance tower remains. In past centuries Putna, even more than Secu and Neamt, was a centre of learning, with important MS-copying, icon-painting, and embroidery workshops. Most important of all, it housed Romania's earliest Orthodox music school, where singers and choirmasters were trained before even printing was in use. Its museum contains striking

embroideries up to five centuries old, as well as ancient icons, early printed books, and church treasures. Even while acting as a fortress and place of refuge in time of invasion Putna carried on its work.

For Romanians, even those not strongly religious, it's almost a place of pilgrimage. The surrounding mountains are lovely enough for anyone to enjoy being here.

Apart from the usual bus services Putna has a railway station with one through train a day from Bucharest via Suceava.

To complete this tour of the Bucovina I must mention two more strongly fortified monasteries. You can reach one, Slatina, by diverting southward from the DN17 at Paltinoasa, on your way back to Suceava from Humor. Unlike Agapia, Putna, Sucevita, Moldovita, and many others, it lies in a rather shallow small valley, a little clear of the main Carpathians. You feel it was founded to do duty as a sort of advance defence post against Turks and marauding Tatars coming from the east.

The other monastery, stone-built Dragomirna, stands majestically beside a stream, which acts almost as a moat, on flat land 14 km directly north of Suceava. Its church is superb, and all its walls all seem to be about 2 m thick. It's much later in date than most other monasteries we've seen. It was founded in 1607 by the Moldavian Metropolitan Anastasie Crimca, who was himself a remarkable artist. Dragomirna's church was built later, by Prince Miron Barnovschi, ruler of Moldavia, in 1627. Crimca's buried in a small church outside the monastery walls. He himelf built it in 1602.

Dragomirna's occupied by nuns, and

their singing's superb. Their lives are organised on the same lines at Agapia. That's true of course of all Romania's innumerable monasteries, though some today have very few monks or nuns. The main difference at Dragomirna is that its buildings are so grand. The only word to describe the Mother Superior's offices in the old buildings is magnificent.

Iasi and Moldavia's Lowlands

Apart from the city of Iasi (known as Jassy in German and several other languages, though the name's actually pronounced Yash) Moldavia's lowlands aren't sufficiently interesting to take you out of your way – unless you have some specialist historical interests.

If you've been in Suceava and are interested in music you may be tempted to go north to Dorohoi and to the museums housed in George Enescu's birthplace, and in the village 14 km further on, where he lived. Formerly called Liveni, it was renamed after Enescu himself. If so, don't bother. The places are hardly worth the effort.

Botosani, 43 km WNW of Suceava, has some reputation among Romanians because it was the birthplace of their beloved poet Mihai Eminescu. But that's not likely to excite foreigners who can't even read Romanian. The countryside anyway isn't specially attractive.

To reach Iasi by car from Galati you can drive the 230-odd km on the DN24. It's a pretty unexciting long run. You go via Tecuci, Birlad, and Vaslui (capital of the county of that name). All have places of historical interest, but nothing likely to grab the ordinary traveller, and certainly no scenery even remotely comparable to what we've been seeing round all Moldavia's and the Bucovina's superb monasteries.

From Suceava the easiest route is probably south on the DN2 to Sabaoani, 12 km short of Roman, where you turn east on the DN28. From Bucharest you simply take the DN2 to Sabaoani. It's 73 km from here to Iasi. The town's served also by fast trains from Bucharest, some on their way to Kiev and Odessa in the USSR via the rail frontier post at Ungheni, 20 km beyond Iasi. The road crossing is at Albita, 65 km southeast. You can fly direct to Iasi from Bucharest.

Iasi's main interest is the astonishing Three Hierarchs (Trei Ierarhi) Church dating from 1639. Its stone walls are covered all over on the outside with an intricate and detailed carved pattern imitated from traditional wood carvings and the elaborate, inter-twined decorations of medieval manuscripts. It's considered one of Romania's most beautiful buildings.

It contains the tombs of several of Moldavia's rulers, including that of Dimitrie Cantemir (1673–1723), an outstanding scholar, whose *Descriptio Moldaviae* tells us a tremendous amount about Romanian customs, history, and even music of his time, and also about the Ottoman Empire. Elected Voivode (Prince) of Moldavia in 1710, he joined the Russian Czar, Peter the Great, in opposing the Turks, was deposed by them in 1711, and spent his remaining years in exile at the Russian court, writing his scholarly dissertation.

If you see nothing but the outside of the Three Hierarchs Church you may well think your journey to Iasi worth the effort. There are other buildings worth noticing however. One is the National Theatre (1896) in Strada 9

Mai, and another the neo-gothic Palace of Culture (Palatul Culturii), dating from 1905. "Culture" may be a dirty word among Brits. Other nations think otherwise. Iasi's Palace of Culture is a superb building. Do go inside, even if only to enjoy the building's architecture – though it also houses all the country's main museums, ethnographic and technical as well as the regional art gallery.

There are a number of other fine churches – the Princely Church (Biserica Domneasca) built by Stephen the Great beside the palace, whose remains have survived, in 1491; the Golia Monastery church (1660); the Galata church (1538); the St Sava (1625); the Cetatuia Monastery church (1625), which reflects the Three Hierarchs' exterior decoration; the Aroneanu (1593); the Sfintu Ioan Botezator (St John Baptist 1635); and the Metropolitan Cathedral of 1833.

For basic orientation in Iasi make for the Piata Unirii. You'll find the Unirea and Traian Hotels in it, with the Continental in Strada Cuza Voda, leading southeast, and the Moldova in Strada Stefan cel Mare to Cuza Voda's right. If you continue down Stefan cel Mare you'll come to the Metropolitan Church, the Three Hierarchs, and the Palace of Culture (1 Strada Palat). The Golia Monastery is in Cuza Voda. The railway "agentie", Tarom's offices, and the Automobil Clubul Roman's Moldavian HQ are all in Strada Lapusneanu leading out of the opposite side of Piata from Stefan cel Mare. Other places of interest are scattered around the town centre.

If you've gone all through this chapter you may feel that Moldavia consists almost entirely of churches and monasteries. If so, remember that they're nearly all set in magnificently picturesque scenery, very well worth seeing for its own sake, even if you don't go into a single one of them. But remember too that these churches and monasteries have not only played a tremendously important part in Romania's past history. Even today, when two generations have grown up with religion officially discouraged, they still have a tremendous impact on virtually everyone's thinking through the Orthodox Church's all-embracing outlook and ethos, even though people themselves may not realise this. However "modern" modern Romanians may want to be they can't easily escape from the ways of thinking they've inherited from the centuries when everyone looked for guidance and leadership in everything they did to the Orthodox Church. I talk more about this in Chapter Twelve.

7. The Maramures

Maramures county is today larger than the Maramures proper. The latter, Romania's remotest corner, is tucked away behind mountains that guard it on its southern, northern, and eastern sides. It's even more firmly isolated to north and west by its frontiers with the USSR and Hungary. We meet no international crossing point till we reach Satu Mare, outside the Maramures proper. The annual average temperature in the hollow's lowest parts is 9.4°C. On the high ground it's 0°. There's no evidence that the tough Romans ever penetrated here (except perhaps occasional traders). Yet the Maramures and the Oas depression lying to its west are as Romanian as any part of the country, and show clear traces of Dacian settlements (Chapter Twelve). The region's handicrafts and its rich musical traditions are considered outstanding even by fellow Romanians. The first books printed in the Romanian language (instead of Latin or Church Slavonic) originated from here.

The Maramures forms part of Transylvania. Geographically, however, and to some extent historically, it has been a separate region. For convenience sake this chapter deals with the Maramures and Oas valleys and the region on the southern slopes of the mountains that shut them off from the rest of Transylvania. This southern area contains the valleys of the Somes and its tributaries and includes the fine towns of Baia Mare, capital of Maramures county and Satu Mare, capital of the county with the same name.

The road journey into the Maramures from the Bucovina is an adventure in itself. From Gura Humorului if, instead of turning east towards Suceava on the DN17, you turn west past Cimpulung Moldovenesc (about 25 km) you can either continue through Vatra Dornei over the magnificent Tihuta Pass into Transylvania (Chapter Nine), or turn north just short of Iacobeni onto the DN18.

This north turn takes you first through a village with attractively-painted houses called Ciocanesti (which amuses Romanians a lot because it's one of their words for "bonking"), then past Cirlibaba village and over the Prislop Pass by the only surface route connecting Moldavia and the Maramures. The road was surfaced and modernised only in 1978. When I drove it in heavy rain in 1977 it was axle deep in mud. To polite applause from watching workers who kept well out of our way we slithered from side to side of the cutting's walls. It's the only time I've had my car covered in mud right up to its door-handles.

From the south there are only two roads over the mountains into the Maramures – from Dej in Northern Transylvania (Chapter Eight) via Cosbuc (followed also by a railway line dating mostly from 1948), and from

Baia Mare to Sighetu Marmatiei. A third road runs from Satu Mare (below), skirts the Gutii Mountains, and turns northeast into the Tisa valley and past Sapinta to Sighetu Marmatiei (below).

The Tisa here is a mountain stream marking the frontier between Romania and the USSR. It later becomes a river larger and longer than the Rhine. After flowing through part of the USSR and then from north to south across Hungary's Great Plain, it finally joins the Danube in Yugoslavia's Vojvodina Province.

The Oas Depression or Tara Oasului (Land of Oas), as the Romanians call it, is a little less isolated and climatically a lot milder than the Maramures proper.

The Maramures, and Oas (which, incidentally, is pronounced like *ash* preceded by a *w* sound) have long been areas where non-ferrous metals, including gold and silver, have been mined. Yet they're renowned for the beauty of their magnificent forests and their mountains. And the inhabitants for centuries past have been highly skilled woodworkers.

Here, instead of the modest little wood-built houses with front verandas traditional in Moldavia, you'll see small houses differently shaped and often with magnificently-carved gateways. More woodcarvings may decorate the houses' exteriors, and lovely tall, whimsical wooden sculptures which look like fanciful totem-poles are occasionally erected in roadside clearings for no better reason than that the locals like the idea. Here, too, needless to say, you'll see many of the all-wooden small churches with tall wooden spires which we've mentioned so far only in isolated examples.

If you're lucky, you may also come on country women weaving superb rugs and hangings and other fabrics on primitive handlooms, in summer often out on the verandas of their wooden houses. They'll be only too willing to sell to you. Don't fail however to get a formal receipt. Export without authorisation (obtainable at Customs) of any handmade goods, of whatever age, is forbidden by law. It's one way of preventing private Romanian owners exporting valuables to obtain foreign currency.

Into the Maramures

The Prislop Pass is the saddle between the Maramures Mountains (Muntii Maramuresului), with a 1848 m peak directly to its north, and the Muntii Rodnei, rising to 2300 m and more, to the south. You descend pretty fast through magnificent woods with a variety of trees to the town of Borsa, spread out along the valley. The region's occupations are divided mainly between mining and agriculture, but there's a "tourist complex" which includes a hotel, tourist chalets, and a fairly rough campsite on Borsa's eastern edge. The mines lie mainly north. To the south you can follow a footpath marked by a blue strip to the Pietrosul Mare Nature Reserve, 2700 ha of Alpine vegetation on the slopes of 2305 m-high Mount Pietrosul in the Rodna massif. Allow a good six hours for the expedition, including picnic halts. There are other attractive paths in the area of the Prislop Pass, reached easily from Borsa's "tourist complex".

For the 80-odd-km drive between Borsa and Sighetu Marmatiei you can choose between the main DN18, which runs close to the Russian frontier and has particularly lovely scenery, including areas of orchards, or the minor road, also attractive, which winds along the parallel Iza valley and takes you through a number of delightful small villages, nearly all with one and sometimes two little all-wooden churches. By "little" I meant that the space inside is that of what we'd call a chapel. The interiors are usually dark, but their spires can be disproportionately high. After the strange characteristics of Moldavian churches the sudden plunge into decidedly Western-style architecture, with very Western spires on Orothodox churches, is disconcerting.

From Borsa you go on down the valley to Moisei, which looks modern. It was in fact rebuilt in 1944 after the Nazis had shot 30 people in one house and set fire to the whole village. Its still-surviving 17th century wooden church originally belonged to a monastery dependent on Putna (Chapter Six).

After Moisei fork left to Sacel, about 20 km away in all from Borsa. Sacel's beautiful wooden church dates from the 18th century. The next villages, Salistea de Sus (Lower Salistea) and Dragomiresti, have their wooden churches too. Bogdan Voda, 15 km from Sacel, was originally called Cuhea. The name was changed because the village is thought to have been the birthplace of Bogdan I, the first ruler of Moldavia (Chapter Twelve). He invaded it in 1359, heading a revolt against Hungarian rule and Catholic pressure. Bogdan Voda's wooden church dates from 1722. Foundations of a 14th century stone church and of a fortified stone dwelling have been found nearby.

Just past the village a turning on your left takes you to Ieud, which has two of the most famous of all this region's wooden churches. One, up on a hill, is believed to date from 1364, which

would make it the oldest of all the buildings of this type. Paintings on canvas by local artists of the 15th and 16th centuries are attached to the interior walls.

Rozavlea, 22 km from Sacel, boasts a church made – unusually – of fir-tree trunks. It dates from 1717. The next village's name, Strimtura (or Strimtorea) Tatarilor (Tatars' Passage), commemorates a ferocious battle against Tatar invaders in 1717. Birsana, 37 km from Sacel, boasts a particularly lovely high-steepled wooden church, again decorated with paintings on canvas attached to its inner walls. The church is believed to have been built in 1390 and moved to its present hilltop position early in the 18th century – but whether from a different position in Birsana or from another village isn't known.

At Oncesti, 6 km further on, the wooden church dates from 1795. Traces of a Dacian settlement have been found here. Oncesti lies only 11 km from Sighetu Marmatiei, the Maramures Depression's main town.

After you've seen one wooden church the rest may bore you to tears. However, if you've ever wrestled with even simple carpentering jobs, you'll find it well worth examining the detailed jointing and brilliant construction techniques which made these very stable buildings possible. How many simple wooden structures survive three centuries of wind and weather as well as these churches have? Unfortunately, you can't always see the details. They're clear however at the re-erected church from Cizer in the open-air section of Cluj's Ethnographic Museum (Chapter Eight).

The wooden churches along this valley between Sacel and Sighetu Marmatiei are the best-known group in Romania. Many self-styled "experts" outside the country (with whom I've sometimes had furious rows) maintain they're the only ones. So I'd better point out right away that the churches I've mentioned are a very, very long way indeed from being unique. The Maramures's total alone runs to 54 (I shall deal with a few more), the rest of Transylvania (Chapters Eight and Nine) has 322, Moldavia (where we've already seen a few) 163, the Banat (Chapter Ten) 21, and Wallachia and the Dobrogea, 202.

It's tragically typical of Western Europe's arrogant neglect of Romania's superb craft traditions that even this tiny valley's churches are known only to rare specialists. This seems one more bit of evidence that Eastern Europe has never really been taken seriously in Britain – certainly not by journalists, and sometimes not even by academics assumed to be specialists. It's our loss.

A few kilometres before you reach Sighetu Marmatiei you join the DN18 on its way southward from there. Sighetu Marmatiei, the Maramures's main centre, is Romania's most northerly town. Its Maramuresean Museum, in Strada Bogdan Voda, illustrates all the region's wealth of handwork – not only every sort of woodcarving, but also carpets, icons painted on glass, masks, clothing, and household objects such as the carved distaffs still used in hand spinning. Strada Republicii has both Catholic and Protestant churches. There's a fine natural park, Gradina Morii, on the town's outskirts, with a poplar claimed to be 350 years old. The town's main appeal however lies in its position at the junction of the Rivers Tisa, Ronisoara, and Iza at the foot of the Gutii Mountains. Its main discouragement, as with too many

Romanian towns, is the jumble of modern factories and unattractive flats outside the centre.

If you leave Sighetu Marmatiei by the road running west, close first to the Iza and then the Tisa, you arrive after 18 km at the village of Sapinta, whose cemetery has become famous for its painted headboards. Unlike the epitaphs usually put on graves, these are colourful (in both senses of the word), truthful, often far from laudatory, and full of humour. They're the work of one man, Ion Stan Patras. The cemetery's very popular with coach tourists.

You can continue past Sapinta through very lovely scenery to Negresti-Oas (37 km), where there's another small handicrafts museum, and Satu Mare (87 km), described below. Oas's area is tiny, and it's hemmed in by the USSR. While there are few points of special interest the whole region's extraordinarily attractive. Unfortunately, there aren't any hotels or well-established campsites where you can base yourself.

To Baia Mare

The main DN18 starts southward from Sighetu Marmatiei, repeating the short section you travelled along from Birsana and the Iza valley. Vadu Izei (Iza Ford), at the two road's junction, has some specially striking carved gateways, and is famous for its colourful local costumes. Desesti, 25 km from Sighetu, has another all-wooden church, as have several villages east of the DN18.

On this road you're driving all the while through magnificently-forested mountain slopes. At 40 km from Sighetu, at the top of the Gutii Pass, you reach a very attractive stopping-place, with a car park and restaurant. It's the starting-point for a popular footpath, not easy going, up to the Creasta Cocosului (Cock's Crest) geological reserve in the Gutii Mountains. It takes its name from the coxcomb rock formations.

There are other popular and very lovely excursion destinations in the Gutii Mountains. One, known variously as Fintina cu Trei Izvoare (The Fountain with Three Springs) or simply Izvoarele (The Springs), is associated with a famous local *haiduc*, Grigore Pintea. That gives it a third name, Izvorul lui Pintea – Pintea's Spring. The word *haiduc* is usually translated "outlaw", which is what these people certainly were in the authorities' eyes. Local folk however regarded them as heroic guerillas bravely fighting oppressive foreign occupying forces – in Pintea's case the Habsburgs (Chapter Twelve). Known to everyone as Pintea Viteazul (Pintea the Brave), he was killed during the 1703–11 anti-Habsburg rising. In snowy winters people come to ski at his springs.

This is another area where you'll find a number of marked paths, some leading to spots where, in summer at least, you can get drinks and snacks. Views from many points are excellent and in autumn the foliage colours glow magnificently.

On the main DN18 we reach Baia Sprie at 17 km from the stopping-place at the top of the pass. Basically, it's a small mining town. But there's a 14th century Catholic church and parish house, paid for by forced contributions from the miners under Hungarian rule. The building erected for themselves centuries ago by the Jesuits is now the modern Town Hall.

Another 10 km brings us to Baia Mare, today the Maramures's county town. Although it's another ancient mining settlement the town today is mostly attractive with its newer parts to the south. Traces of the ancient fortifications which have survived include the Mint Tower (Bastionul Monetariei), down beside the River Sasar, and the Butcher's Tower in Piata Izvoarele.

In Piata Libertatii you can see the Elisabeth House (Casa Elisabeta), built for his wife in 1446 by the great leader and general, Iancu of Hunedoara, whom the Hungarians call Hunyadi Janos (Chapter Twelve). The picturesque Old Inn (Hanul Veche) in Strada 1 Mai, much used by 18th and 19th century travellers, now houses the County Law Courts. You'll find the County Museum (Muzeul judetean) in Strada 1 Mai too. The railway "agentie" occupies the ground floor of a former Franciscan Monastery in Piata Libertatii.

Piata Cetatii, west of Piata Libertatii, holds the 15th century Stephen Tower (or Clock Tower), once part of the town's fortifications. The baroque Sfintu Treime (Holy Trinity) Cathedral, built by Jesuits in 1720, also stands here. You'll find most of the notices inside are in Hungarian.

Baia Mare boasts four good hotels, a railway station with the bus station beside it, and direct air services to Bucharest. The surrounding region is very well worth exploring, whether by car or by bus and on foot. With luck the Tourist Office in Strada Pietrosului towards the river will be able to advise and help you. They can certainly tell you where to find all the region's wooden churches.

To Satu Mare

You can reach Satu Mare from Baia

Mare by the DN1C north of the Somes river, or by minor roads on its southern side. Main-line expresses from Bucharest also link the two towns. Planes fly direct from Bucharest. And, of course, these two county towns are also served by the usual bus routes with stops in intervening villages. A road running west from the town takes you into Hungary. Satu Mare has two good, but fairly small, hotels.

Once here, you're out of the mountains. The Carpathians sweep on northwest into Czechoslovakia and Poland, beyond the Maramures and the Tara Oasului. Here you're in an altogether gentler, flatter countryside, with rice-fields and marshes not far south, close to the Hungarian border. In effect it's part of the Great Hungarian Plain.

Satu Mare's an attractive town, with a specially pleasant centre – the Piata Libertatii and the broad Bulevardul Eliberarii (Liberation Avenue) leading east from it. You'll find almost everything that's of interest in or close to this spot. The two hotels are here. One of them occupies a floridly ornate building dating from 1909. The railway "agentie", Tarom's office, ACR county HQ, and the Tourist Office are all close by. A house where Sandor Petofi, Hungary's great poet, lived in 1847 can be seen at 6 Strada Cuza Voda. The town's population is partly Romanian, partly Hungarian, and partly German in origin.

There's a campsite at Paulesti, 5 km southeast of Satu Mare.

8. The Salaj and the Bihor

After spending a lot of time first in the Dobrogea, where modern coast resorts and the unique Danube delta are the main attractions, then in Moldavia, where you can go from one fantastic monastery to another through splendid scenery, and finally among the wooden churches and equally entrancing friendly Marmaures landscapes, we come now to another perhaps even more exciting part of Transylvania. It's one whose scenery is quite as magnificent as anything we've already enjoyed. Here however you'll also find a lot of fine towns, all set among mountains and hills, with a combination of forests and valleys, wild gorges, and bare high regions, sometimes rocky, sometimes green and grassy, in betweeen.

I'd better start by explaining some of this region's confusing names. The Salaj is the area of hilly "plateau" land south of Satu Mare and Baia Mare, largely enclosed to its north east, and southwest by the River Somes. That's simple.

What I shall call the Bihor is the mountain region east of Oradea which blocks the Carpathian horseshoe's mouth. This is a name commonly given it. It's also the name of the modern county that has Oradea as its capital (and part-name of Hajdu-Bihar county on the Hungarian border's further side). But the Bihor Mountains proper are only a small, southern part of the total clump east of Oradea, and they lie outside Bihor county. Each set

of Bihor heights has its own name – Muntii Padurea Craiului, Muntii Vladeasa, Gilau, Metaliferi, Trascau, and Bihor. Collectively they're also called the Apuseni. The people who live in and around them are the Moti.

For good measure this Bihor region is also sometimes called Crisana, its former administrative title. It's the region where the three Cris rivers rise – Rapid Cris, White Cris, Black Cris – together with all their tributaries. Crossing the modern Hungarian border they combine to form the Koros, which flows into the Tisa, and thence to the Danube.

In this chapter I deal not only with the Bihor/Apuseni mountains, but also with the often very attractive towns that lie on their lower slopes and in the valleys around them. They reflect the great days of Transylvania's 17th–18th century prosperity (Chapter Twelve). The mountains were home too to many of Romania's revered revolutionary peasant leaders.

Many areas were still decidedly remote until the 1960s. Today the ancient folk music, folk traditions, and folk handicrafts of both Romanian and Hungarian villagers still flourish here. My Hungarian musician friends, in fact, come to this part of Romania to recover the old Hungarian songs and dances that have recently become so popular in their own country after being effectively almost totally killed off in Hungary proper by governments intent on being "modern". It was in the Bihor too that Bartok collected many of his traditional Romanian melodies.

But to start our journeying in this part of Transylvania we must go back to Satu Mare and look first at the strip of Romania lying along the border with Hungary, and then at the hilly Salaj.

Satu Mare to Oradea

This is a dull, rather frustrating 123 km stretch. Whether you go by road or rail you're travelling through uninspiring flat land all the way, with enticing hills to your east and the often very attractive low sandhills of Eastern Hungary coming right up to the frontier on your western side. This DN19 route's only advantage is that it allows you to move easily between Oradea and Satu Mare and thence to or from Oas and the Maramures.

Carei, 36 km south of Satu Mare, set in an area of rice-fields and marshes, has a pleasant baroque Catholic church in the town and a lakeside campsite 9 km north of it.

There's a main-road frontier crossing at Petea, some 14 km NW from Satu Mare, and rail-and-road crossing at Valea lui Mihai (Michael's Vale), 57 km SW. And at Biharea, 13 km short of Oradea, you can see the remains of a 10th century earth citadel erected by Menmorut, the first known leader of any settled community in this area following the migratory turmoil of the previous four centuries.

Across the Salaj

A recently re-aligned and modernised road takes you southeast direct from Satu Mare to Cluj, Transylvania's former capital, through the heart of the Salaj. It runs through Zalau, capital of modern Salaj county. The distance

is just over 150 km. The road's Romanian numbering varies between DN1F and DN19A, but you may see it also signposted as E81 in the European Routes system.

Despite this modern road the Salaj is still a lonely area, largely unknown even to Romanian tourists. It's hilly, not mountainous, with extensive woods of very varied trees, and endless pleasant, quiet corners. The region north of Zalau is aptly called Silvania – Land of Woods.

If you want an excuse for exploring the Salaj – though there's no reason why you should need one – try setting out to find and enjoy its 69 wooden churches. They go back to dates as early as 1643. Some are known specially for the height of their spires, others for paintings and decorative carvings at least as remarkable as any you'll have seen in the Maramures. Many have paintings inside similar to the ones you saw earlier. A lot is known about the artists. In old town registers names of local joiners are also often recorded.

Unfortunately, many of the villages the churches stand in – such as Fildul de Sus, Tusa, Ceheiul, Dersida, Horoatu Cehului, Bulgari, Brebi, Hida, Chiesd, Zimbor, Letca, and all the rest – don't make much of a showing (or don't appear at all) on easily-available maps.

Your only solution is to tackle the Tourist information Offices in Zalau and in Simleu Silvaniei, Cehu Silvaniei, and Jibau (or Jibou), west, north, and northeast respectively of Zalau. I can't guarantee you'll find anyone in them who speaks English, though German or French are possibilities. Another snag is that many of these Salaj-region villages don't lie in modern Salaj county (Chapter Thirteen), so the county's Tourist Offices may know nothing about them.

There's one good hotel in Salaj, and one officially-listed campsite on the DN1H road halfway between Simleu Silvaniei and Alesd (on the DN1 that takes you from Oradea to Cluj, below). If you're camping or caravanning you should have no problem in finding friendly folk who'll let you pitch on their land and see that you're supplied with drinking water and similar necessities.

Around the Bihor;
(i) Oradea

The historic town of Oradea is the gateway to Transylvania from the west. The main road from Budapest and the Hungarian Great Plain's capital, Debrecen (via Berettyoujfalu), passes through Oradea (Nagyvarad in Hungarian), and one of the main rail routes comes this way too. The frontier posts of Bors (for the road) and Episcopia Bihorului (rail) lie some 18 km from the town itself.

Oradea's a town with a rich and impressive history. In prehistoric times, as excavations show, it was inhabited at different periods by Dacians, Scythians, and Celts. Near here, as we've already seen, the first ruler of a settled Translyvanian community sited his headquarters. The town's citadel, built in 1114–1131 was destroyed by the Tatars in their devastating 1241 raid, but was rebuilt by the Corvini, as the Romanians call the Hungarian Hunyadi kings (Chapter Twelve).

It was here that Matthias Corvinus, greatest of all the Hunyadis, convened his council. Here he received Stephen the Great of Moldavia's envoys, and made a treaty of peace with the Turkish Sultan Murad. Here, too, in 1514 the great peasant revolutionary

leader Gheorghe Doja, whom Hungarians remember as Dozsa Gyorgy, demanded the abolition of titles of nobility, equality among all men, and sovereignty of the people.

The town lies astride the Cris Repede (Rapid Cris), with a number of fine buildings near the river. Two of the best known however can be seen in Strada Stadionului a little way north. They are the large and elegant Baraque Palace of 1770, designed to recall Vienna's Belvedere Palace, and the so-called "Canons' Corridor" (Sirul Canonirilor), a 1773 baroque building with an impressive groundfloor arcade over 100 m long.

The Baroque Palace contains wonderful 18th century murals and the modern Muzeul Crisurilor, the Museum of the Cris Rivers. Its history, arts, and ethnography sections are all worth seeing. The Roman Catholic Cathedral built in Strada Stadionului in 1780, deserves a visit too.

The ancient Citadel lies on the river's further side, best approached from Strada Iancu de Hunedoara. Five solid towers and parts of the walls remain. The Orthodox Cathedral, dating from 1790, stands in the Pita Victoriei. It's known as "the church with the moon" (biserica cu luna) because of a mechanical device which allows a 3 m globe, half black and half gold, to show the moon's phases.

Popular excursion spots include Baile 1 May (1 May baths), 7 km outside the town north of the DN78 leading to Beius and Deva. Apart from woods and warm springs it includes a Nature Reserve, home to a particularly rare and beautiful water lily. Baile Felix is another warm spring area 8 km out on the DN78. A protected beech and oak forest on the lower slopes of the Crai Forest Mountains (Muntii Padurea

Craiului) forms part of it.

There's a campsite at Baile 1 Mai, and a number of hotels in Oradea itself. Four are graded first-class. The largest and best, the Dacia, faces the river close to the bridge carrying the main road through the town from Bors to Cluj.

Around the Bihor:
(ii) The road to Cluj

If you've never been in Romania before, and cross the road frontier at Bors on your way to, say, Bucharest, your first impression as you leave Oradea is that you're in an extraordinarily beautiful country. You seem to be soaring up and away on a busy but pleasantly fast road through unexpectedly rich and very fertile country, with sudden views ahead of long rolling plains. I still remember very vividly my own first experience of this road. And I can recall very clearly the friendliness of all the people we talked to along the way – even the sunburned lady on her way home from the fields whose cartwheel straw hat one of my companions coveted and insisted on buying literally off the laughing owner's head.

All this is a sudden complete change from the dead flat scenery of the Hungarian Great Plain on your way from Berettyoujfalu through Bors. What doesn't change, though, is the style of the older houses lining the road in many towns and small villages. As on the Hungarian Alfold and in the older parts of towns like Debrecen you see long double rows of single-storey twin-fronted houses, each with a tall double-leaved waggon door leading into the yard the house is built around. These dwellings are very different from the wooden homes you saw in the Danube Delta. They suggest prosperity – maybe only relative prosperity, but something the other regions have never known in all their own history.

The first settlement of any size you pass through is Alesd, 40 km from Oradea. A road on your left leads up into the picturesque Sinteiu valley and the ruins of a castle known locally as Piatra Soimilor – Hawks' Rock.

Another 12 km brings you to Topa de Cris. A turning on your right here takes you to Vadu Crisului (Cris Ford) and the Vintul, Magura, and Corbasca Caves beyond. Vintul, over 6 km long, is Romania's second largest. Magura boasts a tremendous variety of pure limestone "sculpture", including curtains and draperies. Corbasca, only 250 m long, is much visited for the beauty of a quiet side-cave lake which reflects the limestone formations. The surrounding scenery is superb.

Bucea, 18 km further along the DN1, offers a wooden church and a rough turning on your right that takes you to Remeti village and eventually to Stina de Vale (Sheepfold in the Valley), 48 km away and 1100 m up in the Padurea Craiului Mountains. And at Ciucea, 11 km beyond Bucea, the Crisul Repede has cut a beautiful small gorge through the mountains. Here, too, is the former home of the noted Hungarian poet Andre Ady, where many of Romania's best-loved writers and musicians also stayed. From Ciucea an alternative cross-country road takes you north to Zalau and Baia Mare (above).

The village of Poieni, 8 km from Ciucea, is a starting-point for trips southeast into the Valea Draganului, sometimes translated Hell Valley, though Dragan – Dragon or Devil – is the stream's name. There are marked paths to the Valea Draganlui and Vladeasa huts (about 4½ hours). This is one of the many areas where rich repertoires of both Romanian and Hungarian folk music have been and are still being collected. Romanian scholars tend to maintain that, even when living side by side, the two ethnic groups keep their music quite separate. Music brought back by my Hungarian musician friends suggest they often merge.

One interesting result of Celtic settlement in this area some 2300 years ago is local bagpipe music sufficiently similar to Northumberland's for Geordies to have danced spontaneously to Transylvanian tunes when a Romanian friend of mine brought Transylvanian pipers to Bellingham in the 1930s.

Huedin, 13 km from Ciucea, is this region's main settlement. Its 15th century Reformed church has an attractive tower with a wooden lookout/defence balcony. Huedin lies on lower land. But it's the starting-point for exciting excursions high into the Vladeasa and Padurea Craiului Mountains to the south and the Zalau hills to its north. A path marked with a blue strip takes you south to the Vladeasa hut in 2 hours. 1430 m above sea level, it can be your base for many delightful walks.

You reach the Source of the Cris (Izvorul Crisului) 11 km beyond Huedin. There's a wayside restaurant and campsite here. Beyond it you cross the divide between the Cris and Somes valleys.

Another 37 km brings you to Cluj. Romanians today call it officially Cluj-Napoca, stressing the town's Roman origin by adding its Roman name. It has certainly been an important centre at least since the Emperor Hadrian's time (AD 117–128). In medieval times it was known as Clus. In Hungarian today it's called Kolozsvar and in German Clausenburg. As in so many Transylvanian towns you'll hear German and Hungarian spoken here as well as Romanian.

The city's most noticeable feature is its ancient Citadel (Cetatuia), high on a hill and surrounded by parkland north of the River Somes Mic (Little Somes). It has been occupied for at least 800 years.

You reach the town centre by crossing the bridge over the Somes Mic and going straight ahead into Piata Libertatii. Here you'll see St Michael's church (Roman Catholic; 14th–15th century, with a huge 19th century tower). A splendid equestrian statue of Iancu of Hunedoara (or Iancu Corvin, or Hunyadi Janos – take your choice; it's explained in Chapter Twelve) stands in front of it. There's also an art gallery at 30 Piata Libertatii, housed in the 18th century Banffy family mansion, with a small History of Pharmacy Museum at No. 28.

The house where Iancu of Hunedoara's son, the great Hungarian King Matthias Corvinus, was born in 1443 is now 6 Strada Matei Corvin, just northwest of Piata Libertatii. East of the square, in the linked Piata Victoriei and Piata Stefan cel Mare, you'll find the huge Orthodox Cathedral (1921–1933) and the Romanian State Theatre and Opera House. There's a Hungarian State Theatre and Opera House, in a circular building, at 26 Strada 1 Mai, northwest of Piata Libertatii.

The Tailors' Bastion (Bastionul Croitorilor), the best-preserved part of the city's medieval defences, still stands in Strada Facliei. The undemonstrative 15th century Reformed Church, built with help from

Matthias Corvinus, is close to it. Here, too, you'll see a possibly familiar statue of St George killing the dragon. It dates from 1373 and is the same as the one in Prague. The sculptors Martin and Gheorghe of Cluj cast a second copy for their native city.

Cluj's Babes-Bolyai University has its headquarters in Strada Universitatii, leading southwest from Liberty Square. The baroque Piarist church (1724) and the former Piarist High School stand in the same street. Most of the University's modern buildings can be found to the town centre's west.

On your way there you can visit the fine Ethnographic Museum at 21 Strada 30 Decembrie, which runs across Liberty Square's northern edge. But don't miss the museum's open-air section on Hoia Hill, northwest of the city.

It's a lovely collection of old buildings re-erected on an extremely pleasant hillside. Here you can examine all the structural technique of the wooden church brought from Cizer in the southern Salaj (Chapter Seven). One of the most fascinating things in it is its builder's signature. He was none other than Horea, one of the three leaders of the 1784 peasant rebellion (Chapter Twelve). We thinks of "peasants" as horny-handed illiterates. But Horea had already been to Vienna to present a petition to the Emperor before he and his fellow leaders were caught and brutally killed.

There's a lot more to see and enjoy in Cluj, and also in the mountains to its west – to say nothing of the important botanical Nature Reserves at Finatele Clujului 4 km north of the town and Suatu 30 km east, south of the DN16.

Cluj has a number of hotels, both first-class and more modest, a campsite,

and an airport with direct flights from Bucharest. It makes a wonderful base for excursions into both the Apuseni Mountains to its west and the rolling hills of Central Transylvania on its other sides (Chapter Nine).

Around the Bihor:
(iii) Cluj to Deva

We can continue this drive round the Apuseni/Bihor mountains by going through the towns of Turda, Alba Iulia, Sebes (just off our direct route), Brad, Dr Petru Groza, and Beius. From there we'll go either back to Oradea on the DN78 or to Salonta, near the Hungarian border on the DN79 between Oradea and Arad in the Banat (Chapter Ten).

Turda, 30 km from Cluj on the DN1, is another ancient settlement, base for many years of Rome's Legio V Macedonica. Today it's largely industrial, though with a pleasant central area. In Strada Hasdeu a 15th century home of the Bathory family (Chapter Twelve), used as a meeting-place in the 16th century for Transylvania's council of nobles, has become today's History Museum. There's a 15th century Reformed church next to it, and a Catholic church dating from 1500 in Piata Republicii.

Turda's main interest however is as a base for trips to the Turda Gorge (Cheia Turzii). Nearly 3 km long and with almost perpendicular walls sometimes 300 m high, the gorge is an amazing sight. It contains caves inhabited in prehistoric times. It's home to plants that grow nowhere else and to butterflies that can be seen elsewhere only in the Urals and near Rijeka in Yugoslavia. The entire area is a protected Nature Reserve. There's a campsite here, some 450 m up, 12 km from Turda.

The only notable settlements along the DN1's 60 km to Deva are Aiud and Teius. Aiud's claim to fame is as the birthplace of the great Hungarian mathematician Farkas Bolyai (1775–1856). Teius is the railway junction between lines linking Cluj to Deva and the main route from Brasov (Chapter Ten) and Bucharest to Arad (Chapter Nine) and beyond to Budapest, Vienna, and Western Europe. It does however contain Reformed, Catholic, and Orthodox churches from the 13th, 15th, and 16th centuries that are protected ancient monuments.

Alba Iulia's a mainly rather elegant large town – in some ways another Cluj. Like Cluj it's dominated by a citadel surrounded by massive walls. Alba Iulia's fortress however, built by Charles VI of Austria on the principles laid down by Vauban, contains the town's ancient centre. A statue of Charles dominates the third and innermost entrance gate. Inside the Citadel (Cetatea) you'll find the Roman Catholic Cathedral, built to replace a church destroyed by the Tatars in 1241, and the Orthodox Cathedral of 1921–22. There's also a Reformed church in the town, built on the site of a 13th century basilica.

The Batthyaneum Library however is in some ways the Citadel's most important building. In 1792 the Catholic Bishop of Alba Iulia, Ignac Batthyany decided to collect old books and manuscripts, and to house them in a former monastery. The MSS include part of the magnificently ornate 8th century Codex Aureus (the other main part is in the Vatican, while the British Museum has one cover), a 10th century copy of Sallust's Bellum Jugurthinum, and the 15th century Codex Burgundiensis, with superb illuminations. The Library's incunabula include a 1482 edition of Ptolemy's

Cosmographia and a unique early printing of Ovid's Heroides.

Transylvania's Unity Museum (Muzeul Unirii) is also located in the Citadel, in Strada Mihai Viteazul. Its magnificent Sala Unirii, where the union of Transylvania with Moldavia and Wallachia was proclaimed in 1918 (Chapter Twelve), served originally as a gaming room for the Austrian garrison's officers – not very popular with local folk. The museum contains a mass of material relating to the country's unification.

Merely walking through the Citadel area, with its flowers, trees, and grass, is a pleasant relaxation. And there's a lot more to see in the town.

On the purely practical side Alba Iulia possesses two sound hotels in its central area and a campsite on the outskirts. The Tourist Office and the railway booking centre are in Piata 1 Mai and Strada 1 Mai respectively. In Hungarian Alba Iulia's known as Gyulafehervar and in German as Weissenburg or, in earlier days, Alba Carolina (from Charles VI – Carolus Sextus – of Austria) or Karlsburg.

Just south of Alba Iulia you can fork left off the DN1 onto a side road that joins the west-bound DN7, shortening the distance to Deva. Alternatively, you can continue to Sebes, where DN1 and DN7 meet. You can also turn west off the DN1 to explore the mountain range we're driving round. We'll do that later. For the moment we're bound for Sebes.

Despite industry on its outskirts Sebes is still a small town very much in the Transylvanian tradition. Its houses are less grand, and its streets quieter than those of Cluji and Alba Iulia. But it has the same mountain setting and similar history.

In about 1360 local people decided they wanted to replace their large romanesque church with something more modern in gothic style. They got as far as completing the choir in 1382, when they had to turn their attention to fighting off Turkish attacks. The rebuilding was never completed, but the church remains a harmonious whole. It's used by Evangelicals today.

You can also see remains of the town's fortifications in several spots, including two of the gates and four towers. One of the latter, the Student's Tower, commemorates a schoolboy from a neighbouring village. Attacked in 1438 by a Turkish army under Sultan Murad II himself, Sebes decided to surrender. Some of the townsfolk however, including this boy, shut themselves up in the tower and fought till overwhelmed. Those who survived were taken as slaves to Istanbul. After twenty years of captivity the boy finally escaped and wrote a book, published in 1481 (when printing was still very new). "On the Religion, Customs and Villainies of the Turks" by "The Anonymous Writer of Sebes" had run to sixteen editions by 1500 and to twenty-five by 1600. Luther himself wrote a preface to one edition.

Sebes has a single small, but sound, hotel. A mostly poor road running south from the town, the still incomplete DN67C, takes you through very lovely, lonely mountains and over the 2125 m Urdele Pass into Wallachia.

Turning west on the DN7 you pass through Orastie (where there's a convenient campsite 39 km west of Sebes). The town lies on lower ground below the Dacian mountain stronghold that the Roman forces had to storm in AD 106. The stronghold belongs in my next chapter. Our present route takes

us the further 26 km to Deva.

We're in another quiet, typically Transylvanian town. Its best-known building, usually called the Magna Curia (Great Court), was built in 1621 by Samuel Bethlen, Prince of Transylvania (Chapter Twelve). It's the County Museum today. Its collection includes iron age statuettes discovered in a an ancient gold mine at Baia de Cris, some 40 km northwest towards Oradea on the DN76 main road.

Around the Bihor:
(iv) Deva to the Hungarian border

From Deva we fork right from the DN1 to follow the DN76. The scenery becomes even more striking as we cross the Metaliferi Mountains, skirt the Bihor heights, and then cross the pass between the Crisu Alb's valley to that of the Crisu Negru, flowing between the Padurea Craiului Mountains – we set out earlier along their northern edge – and the Codru-Moma heights to the south.

While we admire the scenery today, the peoples who've inhabited this area throughout history have been more interested in its mining possibilities. Soimus, only 5 km outside Deva, was also once a port on the Mures which floated salt from local mines downstream. Brad, 36 km from Deva, is still a mining centre concerned with various ores. Its Gold Museum covers mining throughout Romania and includes items from Roman times. Tebea, 8 km beyond Brad, has remains of a Roman goldmine. Gold and silver ores are still mined at Garabarza, 5 km from Deva.

Romanians however cannot travel in this area without recalling also its close association with the revolutionary leaders of 1784, Horea, Closca, and Crisan (Chapter Twelve), and with Avram Iancu, who played a major role in the 1848 rising. All were born in this region. Villages here have been renamed in honour of Crisan and Avram Iancu. Many towns have monuments honouring them, including places we've already seen, such as Cluj and Deva. It was in Baia de Cris 10 km beyond Brad, that Avram Iancu was found dead in 1872. He's buried in Tebea, 2 km away.

The area's main town, Dr Petru Groza, was named in honour of the man born here in 1884 who founded the Ploughmen's Front political group in Deva during the slump year of 1933 and in 1945, when the Front was a million strong, headed the Government which ended the war with Germany and organised Romania's first postwar election. It's a modern town, laid out on a grid pattern.

From Dr Petru Groza you can drive the 10 km on the DN 76 (Chapter Nine) to Baita village and then do some really tough walking to the Padis mountain hut (9 hours: path marked with a red stripe) at a height of 1280 m. From this base you can reach the extraordinary karst formations known as Cetatile Ponorului (the Ponor Citadels) in 6 hours (blue dot), the Galbena Gorges (Cheile Galbenei: 8 hours, red stripe), and Stine de Vale (Sheepfold in the Valley, mentioned earlier in this chapter: also red stripe, 8–10 hours).

These are long days. It's not all tough going however because you're on high, flat ground much of the way. While not as high as the Eastern Carpathians on the borders of Moldavia and Transylvania, and certainly not as lofty as the Fagaras range and the Bucegi Massif, which

we've not yet explored, the Apuseni tops are largely treeless. The views are superb.

You come to Beius some 10 km beyond Dr Petru Groza. From here a road that's rough in parts takes you right across the Padurea Craiului Mountains to Alesd, which we passed through after leaving Oradea. And at Simbata, 18 km from Beius, you can choose either to continue on the DN76 to Oradea or to fork left on the minor road to Salonta, where you can turn south on the DN79 on quietly flat ground to reach Arad and the Banat (Chapter Ten).

Across the Bihor

Some fascinating roads lead over and through the Bihor's Gilau, Trascau, and Bihor-proper ranges from Turda and Alba Iulia. Some have only recently been completed. Some are still being either built or realigned and rebuilt. Virtually all take you through magnificent scenery.

They're based on the DN75 and the DN74. The former, in the north, links Turda to Dr Petru Groza through Cimpeni along the Aries valley till it crosses the Bihor hills above Arieseni and descends to the Cris Negru (Black Cris) via Nucet, some 165 km in all. In the south the DN 74 makes a northwesterly run from Alba Iulia to Abrud, and then turns southwest to Brad. Its total length is 105 km. The short DN74A links Abrud and Cimpeni.

For anyone who enjoys walking this is an ideal area for day excursions in which you drive to some suitable spot, park, and then explore on foot. Perhaps the best place to base yourself is at the campside just off the DN74A, close to Rosia Montana under the picturesque twin basalt peaks of the Detunatele (below). Most of the area's interest lies in its scenery. It looks magnificent from a car – but infinitely better on foot. If you're tied to hotels Turda and Alba Iulia are your only effective bases, unless you can find friendly private-house accommodation or one of the "inns" not featured in the Ministry of Tourism's list of official hotels (Chapter Thirteen).

From Turda you set out along the road that took you to the Turda Gorges (above) and simply continue straight on. The scenery as you approach Cimpeni, 87 km from Turda, is particularly fine. Its main feature, from early spring till autumn sets in, seems to be a wonderful greenness that I associate most with southern England at its springtime best. In addition, the fields and woods at the right time of year are sometimes sprinkled and sometimes filled with the multi-coloured and varied wild flowers, plants, insects, and butterflies that intensive farmers' sprays and fertilisers have banished from most of Britain. This is true of almost all this area.

From Salciua to Cimpeni this road's scenery is at its best. You reach the village of Scarisoara a little less than 30 km beyond Cimpeni on the DN75. It's at the next village, Girda de Sus, however, that an unsurfaced track turns northward to take you to the lovely glacier cave of Scarisoara. It rises through green landscapes that are almost 1000 m above the sea, yet look as though they might be somewhere in England's southern half.

The Scarisoara chalet stands near the cave, and serves as a possible starting-point for walks to the beautifully-sited Padis chalet, to the wild limestone scenery of the "Ponor Citadels" hidden in their cloak of giant spruces, and to the Galbena Gorges mentioned

above as being possible destinations also from the town called Dr Petru Groza. This whole area is a typical karst "depression".

But there's a very good reason for turning west off it almost as soon as you leave Cimpeni. A side road here takes you to the village of Vidra and beyond to Avram Iancu (Chapter Twelve), the famous leader's birthplace. From Avram Iancu an unsurfaced but reasonably smooth track takes you up to the heights of Munte Gaina, where one of Romania's most ancient and most colourful traditional festivals takes place every third Sunday in July.

Its site is the mountain's summit – or rather flat land immediately below the little summit knoll, and it's called the Maidens' Fair. Here the Moti, as the Apuseni's inhabitants are called, come up from the valleys – still – on foot, on horseback or muleback, and (increasingly) in cars and vans, to meet and talk, eat and drink, and buy all sorts of things offered for sale from innumerable stalls. Pottery, trinkets, cheap jewellery, household goods, tools, religious paintings that are today's equivalents of the older peasant icons painted on glass – all are on sale here.

Proceedings begin at dawn, just after 4 am – which is a good reason for spending the night on Munte Gaina's flat grassy summit, 1486 m up, well above the tree line. They're opened by a group of women playing stirring tunes on the bacium, an enormous wind instrument resembling somewhat an alphorn, but far more lively and agile. After that the fun begins.

In days gone by it was one of the few occasions when the people of this lonely region could meet folk from the other villages nestling in the valleys round the green mountain. Hence, no doubt, the gathering's name.

It's an extraordinarily light-hearted, cheerful occasion, when even at the height of the Ceausescu terror the police seemed able to relax. One afternoon when I was there we'd just been commenting on how smartly the police who'd come to keep an eye on things were turned out, and how helpful and cheerful they were, when we noticed that the copper in charge had found the dawn start too much for him, had rolled himself up in his blanket and thrown himself down on gently sloping ground for a nap.

The next thing we saw was a group of boisterously-laughing local men and women giving their van a bump start by pushing it downhill perilously close to the police chief. It started with a loud explosion right beside his ear. He rolled over sleepily, took the situation in at a glance, waved cheerily to everyone – and went back to sleep. "Would a British Chief Inspector have behaved so nonchalantly in, say, London's Hyde Park?" I wondered.

As evening began to fall, when the younger fuzz were beginning to chat up the local girls, and everyone was setting off home with the purchases they prized, we passed a seven-year-old who'd crashed out in helpless fatigue on his father's saddle-bow. His head shook so violently with every step the horse took on the rock-strewn steep downhill path that I thought it must fall off. But it stayed attached, and father and son rode

cheerfully, proudly, down into the valley.

If you continue on the DN75 past Girda de Sus you'll find that the 15-km-odd section that crosses the pass beyond Arieseni is specially lovely. The road ends by joining the DN76 just south of Dr Petru Groza.

From Alba Iulia the DN74 takes you through the aptly-named old gold-mining town of Zlatna at the foot of the aptly-named Metaliferi Mountains, Zlatna is the Slav word for "Golden". One wonders where the earliest miners came from. They may have been here in Roman times.

The forests beyond Zlatna and the pass that takes you across the Metaliferi's summit and down into Abrud are wonderful. From Abrud you can drive on to Brad, on the DN76 between Alba Iulia and Oradea (above). Alternatively, you can take the DN74A linking road to Cimpeni.

Two or three kilometres from Abrud a side road to your right takes you to Rosia Montana, from where you can reach more striking mountaintop scenery, the famous Detunatele peaks. They're basalt formations made up of prism-shaped columns, one spreads out in a crescent and one stands up like a cone. They're 450 m apart, at altitudes of 1169 and 1205 m.

Rosia Montana itself has remains of Roman mines on Dealul Cetatii (Citadel Hill). And if you want to see a typical Moti village go to Bacium Sasa on a side road running east from the DN74A about 6 km south of Abrud.

9. Central Transylvania

In Chapter One I described the Carpathian Mountains, which make up almost one-third of Romania's territory, as being a sort of horse-shoe lying on its side with the opening facing west. And I said that a separate mountain clump, the Bihor, blocked the horse-shoe's west-facing mouth. So far, we've travelled round the horse-shoe's eastern edge, and round and through the mouth-blocking clump. Now we must look at the northeastern, eastern, and southern slopes leading into Transylvania's inner bowl, and at the land that makes up the bowl's floor. Geographers call it the Transylvanian Depression. That makes it sound a dull region. In fact it's quite the opposite.

First a word of vital history. This is the region where Hungarian-speaking Szeklers were settled almost a thousand years ago by the early Hungarian kings to guard their kingdom against marauders constantly moving westward. The Szeklers had themselves been pushed westward by land-hungry Cumans.

It's also a region where Germans were settled in fortified villages from eight hundred years ago, and where Germans occupying major towns were given special privileges by Magyar kings.

In Chapter Twelve I've tried to outline the innumerable conflicts, internal as well as external, that have dogged the Romanian people over the last thousand years. In Transylvania, alas, they still aren't wholly ended.

Romanians are still smarting from centuries-old maltreatment at the hands of Hungarian landowners, priests, and political potentates. Hungarians still resent having had Transylvania handed over, with all its mineral and agricultural wealth, to Romania in 1918. Yet it remains an excitingly beautiful area. And in my experience the people who live there, whatever their ethnic origins, are wonderfully hospitable and friendly.

Once, in a restaurant where I'd been talking German to the staff while we spoke English among ourselves, I noticed that the little string group that entertained diners had stopped playing as we were finishing our meal, and seemed to be eyeing us a bit closely. When we stood up to leave they struck up Auld Lang Syne.

From Moldavia into Transylvania:
(i) the Tihuta Pass

In Chapters Six and Seven I mentioned the DN17 road that takes you from Suceava towards Cimpulung Moldovenesc and Vatra Dornei, past the turnings to Voronet and Humor Monasteries. But I didn't even approach the magnificent Tihuta Pass which this road crosses to enter Transylvania.

Cimpulung Moldovenesc is always given its full title, to distinguish it from another, better-known Cimpulung in the Southern Carpathians. It's a town that stretches along 10 km of mountain-fringed road, at a height of 621 m. Wood-processing is Cimpulung's main occupation. Its wood museum (10 Strada 7 Novembrie) displays a tremendous collection of wooden objects and utensils, including hundreds of wooden spoons from many countries.

There's a hotel here, and campsites a little outside the town, from which you can explore some magnificent mountain areas and a number of fascinating Nature Reserves.

About 4 hours uphill walk (yellow triangle path), or a drive on a somewhat rough track which starts just east of the town, takes you southward to the hut at 1541 m, below Mount Rarau's 1653 m peak. A further 20 minutes brings you to the staggering rock formation known as Pietrele Doamnei (Our Lady's Rocks), near the mountain's summit. The views are magnificent.

A second track off the DN17, starting just beyond the first, fringes another Mount Rarau Nature Reserve, the Slatioara Secular Forest (why "Secular" no one seems able to explain). It contains virgin remnants of the original forest that once covered much of Moldavia. Spruces and firs, with trunks a metre thick, stand more than 50 m high.

You can also make excursions northward to Deia, 3 km from the town, and northwest to the Mestecanis mountain hut. The direct road northeast to Moldovita (DN17A: Chapter Eight) is also incidentally extremely attractive. It crosses a beautifully-wooded pass. And the DN17 itself, on its way southwest to Vatra Dornei, winds over yet another lovely saddle.

Vatra Dornei's altitude is 800 m. The hilly town park tops 1300 m – as high as Ben Nevis, Britain's highest point. If you're really strenuous you can reach the Giumalau hut to the south at 1600 m in about 6 hours (red stripe). From there another 3 hours take you to the Rarau hut, already mentioned. This is walking you'll not forget.

Vatra lies 30 km from the summit of the Tihuta Pass. On the way there you pass Poiana Stampei, where there's a cheese factory and a protected peat bog covering 400 ha. The Pass itself isn't difficult to drive. Yet the views from near its highest point are staggering, with the Caliman mountains (Muntii Calimani) to your south, and the lonely Tirgau and Rodna ranges, separated by the valley of the Mures Mare (Great Mures), to the north. And as you leave the narrow pass you come to the village of Piatra Fintinele. On open land nearby a gigantic spruce, known as the King of the Forest, is believed to be several centuries old.

Your descent to Bistrita is steep. The town itself, 54 km from the Tihuta, is set among orchards and vineyards and is an attractive spot. Its Piata Centrala has a row of 15th–16th century houses with ground-floor galleries where traders used to sell their wares. It contains also an Evangelical church whose building dates from the 15th century. The County Museum (5 Strada Dornei) is housed in a mid-15th century building. The Jewellers' House belonged originally to Iancu de Hunedoara himself (Chapter Twelve), and was refashioned by the Jewellers' Guild two hundred years after his day. The Orthodox Church in Piata Unirii is the town's oldest building. It dates from 1270–1280. Very uncharacteristically (Chapter Twelve) it contains an ancient organ.

The town's main hotel has been named the Coroana de Aur (Golden Crown) – in honour of Bram Stoker's *Dracula*.

From Bistrita you can turn northeast to Nasaud on the DN17C (the two towns jointly give their name to the modern county). And from here you can drive northeast up the valley of the upper Mures Mare (Great Mures, to distinguish it from its other source-tributaries). It's a colourful drive on a mountain-flanked road that's being extended to join the DN18 below the Prislop Pass (Chapter Seven).

If you go 64 km due west on the DN17, which here hugs the Carpathian horse-shoe's inner edge, you reach Dej. Set among orchards and agricultural land, it's a very different town from the Gheorghe Gheorghiu-Dej in the Eastern Carpathians (Chapter Six). Ancient salt-mines at Ocna Dejului, actually in the town at an altitude of 320 m, have become a small spa today. Salt is still mined nearby. But the town's main industries are timber and farming.

Its central Piata Bobilna contains a 15th century Evangelical church and a Franciscan monastery dating from 1730 with a fine baroque facade and interior murals. A monument to those deported for forced labour during WWII stands in Piata Stefan cel Mare, and a tablet on a little house at 23 Strada 8 Novembrie tells us that Gheorghe Gheorghiu-Dej lived there in 1930–32.

For Romanians however the town of Dej is notable chiefly because it's the nearest main settlement to Bobilna, 20 km west. In June 1437, on Bobilna Hill, just above the village formerly called Olpret and now re-named Bobilna, a great gathering of Romanian and Hungarian peasants, mine workers producing salt and ores from nearby mines, poor townsfolk, and minor country gentry met to do battle with their oppressors, the (mainly Hungarian) big aristocratic landowners, Catholic Church dignitaries, and Szekler and German town leaders (the latter from German settlements described below).

The peasants won the day. But not for long. An agreement between the two sides, concluded at Manastur just outside Cluj (Chapter Eight), conceded most of the rebels' demands. However, their opponents met at nearby Capilna in September and agreed new moves among themselves. They also agreed measures to halt the threatening Turkish invasion (Chapter Twelve). They failed in their second aim. But their plans for defeating the rebellion were entirely successful.

When the revolt flared again in November the peasant side was jointly led by a Hungarian from Buda, Hungary's capital, and a Romanian from Vireag in Transylvania. The aristocracy had the support of the Habsburg Emperor, himself casting covetous eyes on the territory. Cluj, which the rebels had captured, was retaken, and the revolt was ferociously suppressed. But this was only one of many rebellions which Romanians, in particular, recall with bitter pride.

From Moldavia into Transylvania:
(ii) The roads from Lake Bicaz

The main DN15, laid out long before the modern dam created Lake Bicaz (Chapter Six), runs from Piatra Neamt to Bicaz, turns northwest up the valley in which the lake now lies, and then turns southwest at Poiana Teiului village at the lake's northern tip. You're already 450-odd m above sea level here. But the road climbs steadily for some 50 km more through striking highland scenery to the little spa town of Borsec.

It's a beautiful, well-forested spot, which would be totally blissful but for the constant bustle of trucks carrying the bottle spa water all over Romania (where it gets to after leaving the town isn't always clear: almost the only spot I found with a stock of Borsec recently was Agapia Monastery).

A hundred years ago they managed things more quietly. The water was taken on carts across the pass to Toplita in Transylvania. From here it was rafted down the Mures, which sweeps southwest in a wide arc to Tirgu Mures, flows on to Alba Iulia (Chapter 8), then turns west to Deva and Arad (Chapter Ten), and finally joins the Tisa at Szeged in Hungary, close to the Yugoslav frontier.

Coming down from Borsec the DN15 is steep, but not difficult. It follows the Mures to Tirgu Mures. There's a campsite close to Borsec which allows you to sample half a dozen or more mostly easy walks around the town. Despite the altitude you don't have much sense of being in the mountains.

Your second road into Transylvania from Lake Bicaz, the DN12C, is heavily used by tourist traffic. It starts southwest from modern Bicaz, crosses the pass between the villages of Chisirig and Bicaz Ardelean (Transylvanian Bicaz) and, 25 km from Moldavian Bicaz plunges into the spectacular limestone Bicaz Gorge. In places it was so narrow – barely 6 or 7 m – that it had to be widened to take the modern road beside the River Bicaz. The road has been carefully built. Modern coaches can negotiate its hairpin bends without undue problem.

The gorge itself is 300–400 m deep, and the scenery superb. And just as you come out of its lower end you reach Lacul Rosu, the Red Lake, formed by landslides which blocked the River Bicaz in 1837–38. The lake gets its name from the reflection of Mount Suhard's red clay. Petrified remains of ancient firs still project from the lake. Its peaceful waters and the wonderful views attract thousands of tourists. They're catered for with restaurants, a campsite,and so on. There are also marked paths that guide you up the mountainsides to surrounding heights.

Two hours walk brings you to the Lapos Gorges. A yellow triangle marks the path to the Raza Soarelui clearing, where you can follow a red triangle to the Great Suhard and Ghilcos summits. For the Piatra Singuratica hut you follow the red stripe, on a path running below the Haghimas heights to the south. A red dot takes you to high points in the northern Suhard range. But these routes are much tougher, and recommended only for experienced mountain walkers. You should in any case ask about current conditions and weather before setting out.

Other, easier, walks are possible from the Bicaz chalet at the gorge's upper end. They're equally well signposted. If you're not an experienced walker, however, make sure you're wearing comfortable trainers or walking boots and allow a decent margin over and above the stated time.

The road's final descent to Gheorgheni is relatively tame, but pleasant. Gheorgheni's a crossroads of the DN12 from Miercurea Ciuc (below) to Toplita (above) and the 12C (which we're on) - 13C route continuing southwest to Sovata (below). It has a campsite.

The scenery's extremely attractive throughout this region. It's an area where the mountains are of volcanic origin – extinct now,though still active at great depth, as the May 1990 earthquake showed. The River Mures, which flows first north, then southwest, and finally westward to join the Danube, and the Olt, which runs first southwest and then south in a magnificent steep-sided valley cut in the Southern Carpathians (Chapter Eleven), both rise close to Gheorgheni.

From Moldavia into Transylvania:
(iii) The Ghimes and Oituz Passes

We made a diversion from the main road on our way north from Bucharest to Suceava, and came as far west as the region round the town called Gheorghe Gheorghiu-Dej (Chapter Six). Now we must consider the two passes that take us into Transylvania.

The more northerly,the Ghimes, carries the DN12A, whose winding route links Gheorghe Gheorgiu-Dej to Miercurea Ciuc, a distance of 105 km. The Oituz carries the DN11 on its 130-km journey from Gheorghe Gheorghe-Dej to Brasov. Both are scenic in the extreme. But the Ghimes carries less traffic.

Its main attraction is the forest scenery it passes through, though this is mixed at times with modern industry. From Tirgu Ocna (Chapter Six) it climbs the Trotus valley to Doftana (or Dofteana), where there's a forest Nature Reserve, then to Comanesti, 24 km from Tirgu Ocna. Coal and oil are both worked in this area. Romania's oldest oil refinery in fact is located at Moinesti, 10 km northeast of Comanesti on the DJ156 side road which takes you eventually to Bacau (Chapter Six).

At Tirgu Ocna you were already 530 m above sea level, and the recently-surfaced road is climbing all the time. With its industrial sections now behind you the scenery becomes really lovely. Villages are few and far between. You reach the summit close to Ghimes Faget and wind steeply down into the south-flowing Olt's valley at Pauleni Ciuc just north of Miercurea Ciuc. The total distance from Tirgu Ocna is 106 km.

Miercurea Ciuc is an important crossroads on the DN12, which forks from the DN11 some 20 km northeast of Brasov (below). You'll find two good-standard hotels in the town, though I know of no campside nearer than Tusnad (below).

The town has a long, mostly troubled history. For almost a thousand years it has been a major Szekler centre, fought over by Tatars, Turks, and Hungarian and Romanian peasant rebels. Its Miko fortress in Strada Gheorghe Doja (Dozsa Gyorgy in Hungarian – a Budapest street and metro station carry his name) was built by Miko Ferenc in 1620, destroyed by Tatars and Turks in 1661, and rebuilt in 1716.

Gheorghe Doja, a minor Szekler landowner, was himself born here. He led the major 1514 rebellion against the great landowners (Chapter Twelve), which started because of the aristocrats' maltreatment of the families of men gathered to fight the Turks. Repressive measures taken by the Habsburgs after Mihai Viteazul's murder in 1601 (Chapter Twelve) led to an anti-Habsburg rebellion in 1611. The town's part in WWI, during the German attack on Moldavia and Wallachia through Transylvania, was quite in keeping with its earlier turbulent history. You can see it all in the museum that now occupies the Miko castle.

The DN12 runs northward up the Olt valley, crosses by a low pass between Sindominic and Voslabeni to the Mures, and goes through Gheorgheni to Toplita, a distance of 93 km in all. At Toplita it's renumbered DN15 (see above).

Southward it takes you to Sincraieni and then travels through an important protected peat bog. You can reach Sinmartin by a side road and from here, if you want some really adventurous driving through very fine scenery in the narrow Uzul valley, cross the Eastern Carpathians by a minor pass between the Ghimes (above) and the Oituz (below). After about 25 km more on the DN12 you reach Tusnad, with Baile Tusnad (Tusnad Spa) 7 km further on.

Baile Tusnad, 650 m up, nestles between Mount Baraolt to its west and Mount Ciomad on its eastern flank. Both are covered with huge forests of spruce and firs, with Lake Ciucas at their base. There are restaurants here, along with villas used by people receiving treatment, and a well-placed campsite. Easy walks in the district include one up Mount Ciomad which takes you in about an hour and a half to St Ana Lake, in the crater of an extinct volcano.

You come to the Oituz Pass's summit only 31 km from Gheorghe Gheorghiu-Dej. Like all this region it offers wonderful views all the way. In good weather you see the Carpathians hereabouts in their friendliest, most smiling mood, with a wealth of green meadows and welcoming woodlands. In a cold, snowy winter the barer higher stretches can be pretty bleak, but still decidedly lovely. I felt very sorry for the priest I met one January

on the Oituz Pass. I was snug in a car. It was blowing a blizzard, the snow was deep, and the road abominably icy. But there he was at the roadside, wearing magnificently-embroidered Epiphany vestments, walking from house to isolated house with a posy of dried flowers in one hand, to bless every room in his parishioner's tiny homes.

You reach the pass's summit through a defile 17 km long, with the River Oituz flowing beside the road. Then the road drops steeply to Bretcu, the site of a Roman settlement aptly named Augustia (The Narrows). Remains of a Roman *castrum* (fort) have been discovered here. Bretcu's a forestry centre today.

Another 16 km brings you to Tirgu Secuiesc. As its name indicates – Secu is Romanian for Szekler – this was another major centre of Szekler settlement, where you'll still hear at least as much Hungarian spoken as Romanian. Indeed, until the 1950s you would probably have found it difficult to travel anywhere along these west-facing slopes of the Carpathian horse-shoe's inmost recess without at least some knowledge of Hungarian. People from Britain and other Western countries find it difficult to realise how separately the different ethnic communities in Romania lived till very recent times. There's far more mixing now. But I don't think that change is wholly for the better. Trying to live between two cultures can be very unsettling, even when political uncertainties aren't adding problems.

Since prehistoric times Tirgu Secuiesc (Szekler Market – Kezdvasarhely in Hungarian), at the foot of the Oituz Pass, has been an important trading post. The route it lies on isn't only the way between Transylvania and

Moldavia. It's also one of many roads traders once used to travel between Central Europe, Istanbul, and other parts of the Near East.

Brasov (below) lies 60 km beyond Tirgu Secuiesc. If you wish you can make a detour southward off the DN11 to see Covasna, one of Romania's many well-known spas. It's set, as most of them are, in specially fine mountain scenery. You'll find a number of good hotels and a campsite here.

Inner Transylvania

I consider the four towns of Tirgu Mures, Medias, Sighisoara, and Odorheiu Secuiesc to be Transylvania's innermost heart, wholly enclosed by the Carpathian horseshoe yet clear of it and lying among the rolling lower hills that comprise a third of the country. They form a triangle, tilted slightly westward, with Tirgu Mures at the summit and the other three towns stretched along its base. There are other, smaller towns around them. But these three stand out. Tirgu Mures and Sighisoara, in particular, are outstandingly lovely, but in totally different ways.

Tirgu Mures lies in a very fertile region a little south of the point where the River Mures emerges from a narrow defile. Its wealth of baroque architecture is typical of Transylvania's towns and includes a lot that's specially protected, especially a number of houses in its central Piata Trandafirilor (Rose Square – the Romanians seem obsessed with roses and water-lilies: every town has at least one street or square named after the rose – Trandafir – and bars called Nufarul, The Water-Lily, are even more frequent than King's Heads in Britain).

One end of Piata Trandafirilor is dominated by the huge Roman Catholic church, built for Jesuits in 1750. Its pulpit and altar are specially fine. There's an Orthodox Cathedral in the square too, dating from 1938. Nos. 11, 53, 54, 55, 56, and 58 are listed architectural monuments. The little Apollo Palace theatre at No. 5 has been staging drama and hosting political meetings since 1820. The Toldalagi house at No. 11 houses the modern part of the County Museum's collection. No. 56 is the Old Town Hall. You'll find the Tourist Office at No. 31.

The magnificent Palace of Culture forms part of this lovely town-centre ensemble but is actually in Soviet Heroes Square (Piata Eroilor Sovietici), a southwest continuation of the already vast Roses Square. It contains a fine concert hall with a notable organ, a number of stained-glass windows illustrating scenes from history and legends, the city's art gallery, and a splendid Hall of Mirrors measuring 40 m by 8 m. Its facade is decorated with mosaics. The Palace of Culture was completed in 1913.

Inside the old Citadel (5 Piata Bernady Gyorgy), constructed in the 15th century, enlarged between 1602 and 1650, and restored at various times since then, you'll find an Evangelical church that was built for Dominicans in 1422, and later taken over by Franciscans before passing to Protestants in the late 16th century. The Diet (governing council) of Transylvania met thirty-seven times in this church at various dates.

Strada Doicesti, northeast of Piata Trandafirilor (you reach it along Strada Avram Iancu), contains two Orthodox churches, one built in stone and one in wood.

The most important of all Tirgu Mures's fine buildings, however, is probably the Teleki Reference Library in Piata Bolyai. The building dates from 1804. Its collection was begun by Count Samuel Teleki, a member of a family famous in Transylvania's and Hungary's history, who was Chancellor of Transylvania from 1791 to 1822. The library's main treasures run to books produced by famous early printers whose names are still household words to modern printers and publishers – Elsevier, Plantin, and Bodoni – as well as copies of a history of the theatre printed in Venice in 1497, Jansson's Atlas Major issued in Amsterdam in 1657-82, the great 33-volume French Encyclopedia of 1780 to which Rousseau, Voltaire, Diderot, and others had contributed, and a Tibetan Dictionary compiled by a leading Romanian orientalist and published in Calcutta in 1834.

All sorts of famous historical literary figures and scholars have made Tirgu Mures their home. They include Bolyai Farkas (1775–1856), the Hungarian mathematician who was one of the founders of non-Euclidean geometry, and his son Janos, himself a noted mathematician; Avram Iancu, one of he 1848 revolution's leading Romanian figures; and Petofi Sandor, the great Hungarian poet. Petofi stayed here in 1849, immediately before leaving for Albesti, where he was killed fighting with the revolutionary troops.

Tirgu Mures has had the same sort of tormented history as most of Transylvania. Even after the recent revolution which removed Nicolae Ceausescu from power it was still in a very disturbed state. I was in Romania – happily (for me) not in Tirgu Mures itself – during the riot early in 1990 in which a number of people were killed. Apart from the deaths, the most disturbing feature of the riot – for me – is that no proper explanation of what happened and why has ever emerged. Totally different accounts were provided by media and officials in Romania and in Hungary. It's an unhappy situation.

Tirgu Mures boasts several good hotels and a pleasant campsite on the outskirts. As a bus centre it's very useful, but somewhat off the main rail routes.

Medias lies 93 km from Tirgu Mures, at the western corner of our triangle. You can reach it by taking the DN13 south to Sighisoara and the DN14 west to Medias – if you don't mind giving Sighisoara a miss for the moment. At Medias you're in a colourful smaller town, surrounded by hills with extensive vineyards – Medias's crest is a bunch of grapes. The town itself, typically Transylvanian in its architecture, stands on a hill, topped with something we've not seen till now but which we'll find is common in this region (below) – a church surrounded by a fortifying wall and towers, raised in the 14th century. One of the towers, 74 m high, leans a bit. It was built in 1450 and had a clock showing the moon's phases added in 1880. Vlad Tepes was imprisoned here for a time by Matthias Corvinus after they'd fallen out in 1476 (Chapter Twelve).

Medias suffers from having Copsa Mica only 13 km to its southwest. An English-language guidebook published in Romania in the early 1970s, when poorer countries were still intent on aping the Western Joneses' metallurgical and chemical industries, talks eloquently and encouragingly about the "strange black castle" of its carbon black works (founded 1936), its sulphuric acid factory, its vinyl polychloride works, Romania's first, and "the new, modern dwellings, and social and cultural establishments of this town of chemistry".

Today, as you leave Medias, you begin to be very aware indeed of the carbon black factory and all Copsa Mica's other horrors. The whole countryside has been turned black, and the chemicals are poisoning thousands of people, particularly children. The vegetation's suffering too. Matters aren't helped by the fact that Copsa Mica lies in a rather small valley, constricted by hills. I was horrified when I saw the region recently after a gap of four years or so.

The DN14 goes through the town on its way from Sighisoara to Sibiu (below). But you can avoid its sights and smells by taking the southbound side road from Sighisoara to Agnita.

Sighisoara's Hungarian name is Segesvar. In German it's known as Schassburg. Its old citadel area, high on a steep bluff overlooking the Tirnava Mare, which joins the Mures at Teius, north of Alba Iulia, must surely count as one of Europe's loveliest urban areas. What's specially charming is that so little modernisation has been even attempted in the last few centuries. Apart from electricity and telephone cables, and maybe a few notices, the citadel's appearance can have changed little in the last five hundred years or more.

One perfectly ordinary-looking house, for instance, has a modest plaque on it saying that Vlad Dracul, Vlad Tepes' father, lived there from 1431 to 1435, during a period when he had been ousted as Prince of Wallachia – which means that Vlad Tepes was almost certainly born in that house (Chapter Twelve). For a time the town formed part of the Prince of Moldavia's domain.

The picturesque 60 m-high Clock Tower featured on this book's cover guards the citadel's main entrance. It dates from the 14th century. You can reach it up a long stairway with 172 steps from the attractive baroque square on flat land south of the hill. The tower houses a history museum which includes some icons painted on glass, a traditional craft once important in Transylvania and not totally forgotten even today. The view from the tower's lookout balcony is very striking. A mechanical device was attached to the clock in 1648 which caused a figure a metre high representing each day of the week to appear at midnight. It seems not to have survived to our day.

The former 13th century Dominican monastery church stands in Piata Maior Isakov close to the tower. Its oriental carpets, baroque altar, and bronze font from 1440 are worth seeing. If you have the strength to struggle to the top of the hill you can also visit the basically 14th century gothic Cathedral.

The Skinners' (Cojocarilor), Tailors' (Croitorilor), Jewellers' (Giuvaergiilor), Butchers' (Macelarilor), and Shoemakers' (Cizmarilor) Towers form the main remains of the citadel's fortifications.

The very pleasant baroque square that the staircase starts from was built after 1676, following a destructive fire. A lot of damage had already been done by a 1668 earthquake.

There's an Orthodox Cathedral on an island in the River Tirnava Mare north of the Citadel, a sound hotel in Strada Gheorghe Gheorghiu-Dej, a little northwest of the baroque square, and a campsite on the town's outskirts. Romania's excellent Tirnava wines come from the region round

Sighisoara. It's a great pity they're not better known in the West. With luck however you'll get a chance to sample them fully while you're in or near Sighisoara. The town's modern suburbs and factories are something most visitors will want to avoid.

The last of our "inner Transylvanian" towns, Odorheiu Secuiesc (Szekelyudvarhely in Hungarian), lies 50 km east of Sighisoara. You get there by a side-road that forks left about 10 km out of the town from the DN13 which links Tirgu Mures and Sighisoara to Brasov. You travel through the town of Cristuru Secuiesc (Szekelykeresztur).

Odorheiu's very modest compared with the somewhat dusty glory of Sighisoara's citadel area. Its main interest is simply that it was once a major Szekler base. A Reformed college was founded here in 1633, on lines similar to those created in Hungary, some of which (eg, at Debrecen and Sarospatak) still flourish today. But it was closed years ago. Traces of a citadel can still be seen. It was built on the site of a Roman *castrum*, and turned into a castle by Stephen Bathory when he was Prince of Transylvania (1479–93: Chapter Twelve). But that was destroyed in 1706.

If you've already seen Sighisoara and want an alternative route to Tirgu Mures (or vice versa) you can take the DN13A to Sovata, some 38 km from Odorheiu and 45 from Sighisoara. Sovata's one of Romania's best-loved spas, with a very picturesque setting. In addition, it offers four good hotels and a campsite.

German Transylvania and the village citadels

In the Middle Ages, almost from the time that the Great Migrations ended and Central and Eastern Europe's communities began to settle to a more sedentary life, merchants from what is now Germany had started travelling everywhere and selling their wares to whoever would buy them (Polish motorists are doing the same today). In time the great feudal landowners sometimes saw financial advantages for themselves in the trade such men created and encouraged them to settle in towns. They were given charters setting out their rights and privileges.

This was what happened in the southern part of what I call Inner Transylvania, on the north-facing slopes of the Southern Carpathians, at towns like Sibiu and, more particularly, Brasov. German merchants settled in many other Transylvanian towns and indeed elsewhere. But what made this southerly part of Inner Transylvania special was that from the 12th century on large numbers of other German settlers from Saxony were also encouraged to come and live here. They were given land by the Hungarian kings who then controlled Transylvania (Chapter Twelve) on condition that they established small fortresses to deter raiders.

The result was scores of "village citadels" and fortified churches, such as the one already mentioned at Medias (Medgyes in Hungarian). Scores of them are still there today – and attractive and fascinating they are. I can't mention them all, any more than I've been able to tell you about all Romania's wooden churches or all its monastery-fortresses. And there seems to be no book in any language that deals with them.

The most northerly appear to be located at Bazna and Bagaciu, west and east respectively of the DN14A north of Medias on its way to Tirnaveni, another chemical industry centre. There are a further eleven in the Tirnava valley either side of Sighisoara. Axente Sever and Biertan are particularly striking and easily accessible.

Axente Sever is yet another of Romania's villages renamed in honour of a great man connected with it – in this case an army commander in the 1848 revolution (Chapter Twelve). Its little church was built in the 13th century. In the 15th a massive tower with a defence-lookout platform was added and the whole complex surrounded with a wall that had storerooms and living quarters built into it. Unfortunately it's only 3 km distant from Copsa Mica, beside the DN14.

You'll find Biertan 9 km south of Bratei on the DN14, 6 km from Medias and 33 from Sighisoara. Here the church stands solidly on top of a hill in the village's middle, with a wall and a high tower close to it. Tower and church both have arrow slits. Another wall on lower ground is provided with a high entrance tower and a barbican with another tower. It's quite an elaborate little fort, with the church towering above the entire complex.

Saschiz, beside the DN13 about 16 km east of Sighisoara, has another fortified church. Others on or close to the DN14 west of Sighisoara and the DN13 to its east include (travelling west to east) Seia Mica, Valea Viilor (Valley of the Vines), Mosna directly south of Medias, Laslea, Apold south of Sighisoara, Crit, and Bunesti.

If you continue past Mosna on the side road leading south into the hills from Medias you come to a T-junction which takes you westward to Altina

and eastward to three good examples around the little town of Agnita.

Rupea, some 80 km southeast of Sighisoara on the DN13 leading to Brasov (below), allows you to explore the ruins of a village citadel that isn't just a fortified church. In fact, there are the remains of three impressive stone fortresses built here during the 12th, 15th, and 17th centuries. Scrambling up the hill and over the ruins is fairly strenuous however.

About 2 km northeast of Rupea, on a well-surfaced side road, you'll find an attractive fortified church at Homorod, with two more examples at Cata and Drauseni much further up the Homorod Mare's valley (on a somewhat dicey road), and another on the DN13's southern side at Ungra, about 5 km beyond Rupea.

Ungra lies in the Olt valley, after the river has emerged from the defile at the end of the northward loop it makes around the Persan Hills northwest of Brasov. Another long string of these fortified churches can be found on the Olt's northern side as it flows roughly E–W at the foot of the north-facing Southern Carpathians' Fagaras range. When the Olt turns south to cut its magnificent long gorge through the Carpathians these church-forts continue westward to points south of Sebes (above).

Pianu is the most southerly, with others close to Sasciori and at Miercurea Sibiului (beside the DN1), Ocna Sibiului, Sura Mica, Sura Mare, Rosia, Virpar, Nocrich, Marpod, and Chirpar are strung out in the hills north of Sibiu. Cisnadioara, Cisnadie, and Bradu lie to its south. Cincsor, Cincu, and Dealul Frumos lie further east, north of the DN1 between Brasov and Sibiu. You can reach them by a side road going north from the village of Voila, 73 km west of Brasov and 8 km from Fagaras town (below).

The most famous however lie close to Brasov itself. You'll find Codlea and Ghimbav on the DN1 to the town's west, and Cristian and Risnov to its southwest, on the DN73 leading to Cimpulung (the one in Wallachia, not the Cimpulung in Moldavia – Chapter Six). Risnov's jagged walls high on a hill above the road look spectacular as you drive by. They're even more impressive when you climb among them.

Haghig and Maierus lie beside the DN13 north of Brasov and, most visited of all because they're easily accessible to coach parties, Harman and Prejmer lie northeast. At Harman and Prejmer, surrounded by flat land, you get a good idea of the way the walls round these churches were built to house families and their possessions when they needed shelter from invaders. They give a literal meaning to the old German chorale *Ein' feste Burg ist unser Gott* – A mighty fortress is our God.

The churches inside these little fortresses are Evangelical. Many contain good tracking organs – centuries ago the Transylvanian Germans were famous organ-builders – and wonderful carpets. Weaving oriental-style carpets was another local speciality. Till the 1950s you'd have heard little but German spoken in the villages (you can still manage very well with it today). The Transylvanian Saxons still wear their own traditional costumes. But their lives today are far more mixed with the towns than they used to be.

Brasov and Sibiu – and the mountains between them

It's time for us to have a look at the towns of Brasov and Sibiu, and at the road between them. After that we'll go into the hills above them – the Fagaras range that contains Romania's highest mountains. This is part of the area of Romania that draws more visitors than any part of the country except the coast.

Brasov today is a mixture of tourist town and major industrial centre. It's not only a county capital. It's also regarded as the chief city of modern Transylvania. If you arrive by one of the international trains from the West it seems to lie on flat land. Inside the town however you feel it's dominated by massive mountains to the south, with lower but still impressive hills immediately north, inside the present city's boundaries.

Brasov's main tourist sights are well known. The lofty Black Church, so-called because of a 1689 fire, features in innumerable photographs. Evangelical today, it's famous for its excellent organ and its collection of oriental carpets. Its building began in 1389 and was completed in 1477. A statue of Ioan Honterus, Brasov's renowned 16th century musician and man of letters (the Romanians always describe him as a "humanist") stands outside the church. After studying in Vienna and living in Cracow in Poland and Basel in Switzerland he returned to Brasov in 1533 and established a printing press there. The Hungarian record company Hungaroton's excellent LP (SLPX 12047) includes some of his music.

The old Council Hall (Casa Sfatului) in Piata 23 August, rebuilt after the 1689 fire, holds the modern country museum today, and the Hirscher House, built as a merchant's home in 1545, serves as a tourist restaurant today under the name Cerbul

Carpatin (Carpathian Stag – Hirsch is German for stag).

Remains of the town walls hurriedly erected in the 1420s after the town was captured by a Turkish raiding party in 1420 still stand. The Weavers' Bastion (Bastionul Tesatorilor), best preserved of the city's towers, today houses a museum devoted to the fortifications of the town and of the Tara Birsa (Birsa Country) – the plain north of Brasov. The standard coach tour will show you all the main foritification remains.

The Schei Gate and the Ecaterina Gate lie south of the old town centre. The Schei district was for centuries the area occupied by Romanians, who were allowed into the town only at certain times of the day (even today Romanians are still actively resentful of this). Brasov, which the Germans themselves called Kronstadt, was a free city (ie, not controlled by a feudal lord), whose ruling council could make their own laws – and did.

The Schei had its own fortifications, its own school (one of the first to teach in Romanian: it houses a museum today) and, of course, its own (Orthodox) church. St Nicholas's (Biserica Sfintu Nicolae), originally built in 1399 to replace a wooden church dating from 1292, is still there. For a long time it served as a centre of Romanian anti-Habsburg struggle. Its clock was presented by the Czarina Elizabeth of Russia in 1751, when Russia was looking to expand southward. Brasov's oldest Orthodox church however, St Bartholomew's, lies well northwest of the town centre, in Strada Lunga. It dates from 1260.

If you go up on Citadel Hill (Dealul Cetatuia), north of the town centre (the Carpati Hotel looks straight at it), you'll find that the old citadel houses a modern restaurant catering mainly for tourists.

The railway station lies north of the town centre, but the railway's central booking office is in Strada Republicii, east of the Black Church. The Tourist Office is round the corner from the Carpati Hotel in Strada 7 Novembrie. Several other modern hotels provide sound accommodation in Brasov's central area. There's a campsite near the citadel. You can fly to Bucharest from Brasov in less than an hour.

There's so much to see in the area surrounding Brasov that I've had to treat the mountains separately. I've already mentioned various village citadels and fortified churches. Here I propose to consider only the road that runs west from Brasov to Sibiu, part of the main DN1 linking Bucharest to Oradea, and some of the spots reached easily from it. Buses ply regularly between these major towns and there are also strategically-located stations.

The distance from Brasov to Sibiu is 145 km. In the first 30 km you pass Codlea, mentioned above because of its citadel, and cross the low Persan hills. Another 20 km brings you to Sercaia, famous for the Narcissus Glade 8 km south of it, a large hillside area covered with narcissi blossoms in late May-early June. It's reached by a motorable road.

The town of Fagaras, 15 km beyond Sercaia, boasts a pretty solid urban citadel-fortress on flat land. It sheltered Prince Mihai Viteazul's family during the battles he fought in Moldavia and Transylvania before the short-lived unification of the three principalities in 1599–60 (Chapter Twelve). The Orthodox St Nicholas church was built in the 17th century by Constantin Brincoveanu himself

(Chapter Twelve). The Reformed church dates from 1715. Modern Fagaras, is another chemical-industry centre.

8 km beyond the town you come to Voila, where a side-road takes you north to the fortified village churches of Cincsor, Cincu, and Dealul Frumos. Simbata de Jos (Lower Simbata) is the first of several villages from which you can reach mountain huts and "tourist complexes" high in the Fagaras range to your south. Six peaks in the Fagaras top 2500 m, and thirty lie between 2400 and 2500 m. Moldoveanu, 2543 m. is the highest. Most of the huts, however, apart from the one in the Podragul glacial hollow, are positioned at heights between 1200 and 1500 m.

From Simbata de Jos, where there's a railway station (10 km from Fagaras), you can walk or drive (by a side road) the 15 km south to Breaza (another village citadel). It's a four-hour walk from here to the Urlea hut (1535 m: blue triangle path). The same side road takes you to a "tourist complex" at Simbata de Sus (Upper Simbata). From here you can walk to the Valea Simbitei hut (3 hours: red triangle).

A well-surfaced side turning from Ucea de Jos (23 km from Fagaras) takes you the 10 km to the chemical-industry town of Victoria (pop. 12,000). From here you can walk the 6 km across the hills to the Arpas hut. Or you can get there from Arpasu de Jos (railway station: 5 km or so beyond Ucea), either by walking or by driving part of the way on a somewhat rough track. The walk from here to the Podragul hut is reckoned to take 6–7 hours in summer.

The scenery in the Fagaras is mostly much wilder than anything we've seen so far, except in the Turda Gorge and on Ceahlau. But it's magnificent walking country.

If you want to experience it in more comfort (which isn't quite the same thing) you can turn south for a few kilometres on the newly-constructed DN7C leading south from 3 km beyond Arpasu de Jos to Curtea de Arges in Wallachia (Chapter Eleven). On this winding highway you've Mount Moldoveanu rising to 2543 m to your east and Virful Negoiu (Mount Negoiu) soaring 2235 m to the west, while you and your car reach 2045 m. It's Romania's highest road. You come to glacial Lake Bilea after about 30 km. It's set in bare, rocky scenery quite unlike the warm, friendly, forest-covered Eastern Carpathians. It lies 2034 m above sea level, with a large chalet on an island. This is the starting-point for more magnificent mountain walks.

Back on the main DN1 a further 35 km takes you to Sibiu, through Porumbacu de Jos, Avrig, and Selimbar villages. The railway line from Brasov follows the same line.

Sibiu's a beautiful and colourful old town, surrounded by the usual rather unattractive suburban factories and modern flats. Driving in from Brasov it's fairly easy to bear right as you enter Piata Unirii into B-dul N. Balcescu for the linked Piata Republicii, Piata 6 Martie (formerly Piata Mica – the Small Square), and Piata Grivitei. Most of what you want to see lies in or close to this open, airy hilltop area, where flower beds and flower sellers add more colour to the fine old painted houses. Though almost 400 m above sea level it can be extraordinarily hot in summer here.

If you've not seen them already in some of Hungary's Great Plain towns, you'll be struck by the odd-shaped windows let into many houses' roofs. They're shaped rather like eyes, and you feel you're being watched. Walk back to the squares as soon as you've managed to find parking space.

I'd recommend starting in the middle of the open area, in the Piata 6 Martie. You can easily pick out the old Council Tower, part of the 16th century defences, standing between what was originally the Town Hall (now Sibiu's Town Museum) and a Catholic church. At No. 20 you'll find a fine arcaded building, once the Furriers' and Skinners' Halls. No. 2 was originally the Butchers' Hall.

The little square's most-visited spot however is the Scara Fingerling (Fingerling Ladder), a long flight of steps connecting the upper citadel to the town's lower artisan area in Piata Aurarilor (Goldsmiths' Square).

You'll find the Haller House, with its ornate entrance at No. 10 Piata Republicii, and the vast, very well laid out Brukenthal Museum at No. 4. It's a large baroque building, which houses a superb display of paintings that include works by Rubens, van Dyck, Dirk Bouts, David Teniers the Younger, Lucas Cranach the Elder, Titian, and all sorts of Austrian, Italian, Transylvanian, and modern Romanian masters. Its basis is the personal collection made by Samuel Brukenthal, Governor of Transylvania from 1777 to 1787, during the period of Habsburg rule (Chapter Twelve).

The museum's content isn't by any means limited to painting. You can also enjoy a very good, but more limited, folk handicraft section which includes work done by Romanians, Hungarians, and Saxons in Transylvania. The library holds a number of priceless early books and an excellent collection of old Transylvanian newspapers.

Piata Grivitei contains a large 14th–15th century Evangelical church with a notable range of over sixty memorial tablets inside, recalling famous people buried in the church. The Chapter House stands beside it. The 15th century Old Town Hall, the baroque Mansion with the Caryatids (they support the balcony over its entrance), and the modern (1906) Orthodox Cathedral can all be seen in Strada 1 Mai, which leads southwest out of Piata Republicii.

In Strada Cetatii, southeast of the square (go down Strada Gheorghe Lazar past the gardens) you'll find spread out a row of old bastions forming part of the former fortifications – the Haller, Carpenters', Potters', and Arquebusiers' Towers, together with remnants of the town walls. The lower town is less obviously colourful and picturesque. But it contains a number of charming small craftsmen's houses.

Sibiu offers several first-class hotels (much used by coach tourists in summer). There's a railway station north of the town, and an airport with direct flights to Bucharest. Buses (from close to the railway station) serve in particular the many excursion points in the town's surroundings.

These are numerous and interesting. At Dumbrava Sibiului, for instance, in the town's southwest suburbs, there's not only a magnificent oak forest but also an even more staggering Museum of Village Technology.

I find it one of Romania's outstanding attractions. Here you can see all the skills of a non-industrial nation, accustomed to living in small, mostly self-contained, self-supporting communities. Even though water power is exceptionally plentiful throughout Romania's hill and mountain regions no one thought of mechanising their handwork. As a result, it's not just the country people's technical skills you'll find so admirable in the museum. It's also their taste. They took time to produce things they'd enjoy living with as well as using.

The road to Dumbrava Sibiului continues to Rasinari, 11 km from Sibiu. Here there's a famous open-air museum displaying a mass of old buildings and their furnishings, together with a school of popular art, where the old handicraft traditions are preserved.

The road goes on another 20 km past Rasinari to Paltinis, a small summer and winter resort, where there's a campsite, "bungalows" (we'd call them chalets) which you can rent, a restaurant, and a small inn. At Paltinis you're already at 1430 m altitude, and the place is an excellent starting-point for more walks, not in the Fagaras but in the range's westward extension, the Cibin and Lotru mountains. I won't start trying to detail them. I hope those I've already mentioned elsewhere will have whetted your appetite sufficiently to make you want to go to Paltinis and get maps and details there.

Aother out-of-the-way base for excursions is the tiny village of Sibiel, which you reach by taking the DN1 westward towards Sebes and Alba Iulia (Chapter Eight) and forking south onto a very minor road at km 334.5 (that is, a little over 20 km from Sibiu: the kilometre stones are marked with distances from Bucharest). It's signposted for Saliste, but you go on through to Sibiel. There's also a railway halt here, and you can walk or drive from here or from Saliste to

spots like the Fintinele (Fountains) hut, 1257 m up in the Cibin Mountains.

For me, however, much as I love walking. Sibiel's overpowering attraction is its tiny, madly over-crowded gallery of icons on glass. I've hardly dared to do more than mention in passing this form of Romania's – and indeed much of Central Europe's – folk art. It flourished in many remote spots, and the best of the work was produced mainly in the 17th, 18th, and 19th centuries, though it was known as early as the 14th and still exists in a rather debased form today.

If you've kept your eyes open in some of the museums I've mentioned – Sibiu's Brukenthal, for instance, and Bucharest's National Folk Art Museum – you'll have seen some very fine examples. Sibiel's may not be of the same standard. But seeing whole walls totally covered with excellent peasant icons is quite overwhelming.

The Dacian and Hunyadi homelands

Before we go back to Brasov and explore the high Fagaras and the superb Bucegi Massif south of the town we must explore one more corner of the Carpathians – the remote, lovely region where Trajan finally defeated the Dacians, and the corner of Transylvania which gave Hungary its Hunyadi kings. The area involved lies immediately south of the road between Sebes and Deva (Chapter Eight).

Orastie, 58 km west of Sebes, 25 east of Deva, is the gateway to an extraordinarily lovely, lonely mountain area, the Muntii Sebesului. It's lower in height than the mighty Fagaras ridge and the Cibin Mountains to its east. Much of it is wooded, and seemingly fertile. Two thousand years ago it was heavily populated (by the standards of the day). Yet today it appears empty. The long-planned road running up the River Sebes's valley south from Sebes, east of the Sebes Mountains, is still incomplete. It was on these Sebes heights that the Dacian kings built their capital.

If you take the side road south from Orastie you come to the first Dacian citadel at Costesti, 18 km away, with others at Blidaru (22 km), Piatra Rosie on the edge of Luncani village (30 km), and Gradistea de Munte (39 km). It was in fact a whole series of fortified points surrounding the royal city of Sarmizegetusa, which had a fortress covering nearly 2 ha in its centre. Blacksmiths', joiners' and potters' workshops have been excavated, but the work is not complete and indeed appears to have been abandoned. The settlements cover an area of some 150 sq km. Given the degree of wealth and technical ability that this reveals, the Emperor Trajan's obvious pride in having defeated the Dacians is understandable – as is the Romanians' at being the descendants of Romans and Dacians.

Oddly enough, little has been done to help visitors to the area. You can camp at Orastie, but there's no hotel there, and no "interpretive material", even in Romanian, to help you understand and explore the region. Orastie itself is a pleasant little town, with a 15th century citadel and an Evangelical church built in 1560.

There's another spot called Sarmizegetusa, 17 km southwest of Hateg on the DN68 making for Lugoj (Chapter Ten). Hateg itself lies some 40 km south of Deva, via Simeria. This second Sarmizegetusa is the remains of the city founded by Trajan to supersede the Dacian stronghold. It lies on flat ground: the Romans disliked mountain living almost as much as they distrusted sea travel. You can still see remains of its fortifications, of the forum (market place), amphitheatre, College of the Augustales (priests who conducted worship of the Emperor), and private dwellings outside the walls.

A second massive fortification, some 50 km north, via Hateg (DN68) and Calan (DN66), brings us closer to modern times. This is the massive Hunyadi castle at Hunedoara. It stands on an impressive steep bluff dominating the land around. It contains a fine Knights' Hall, with a Council Chamber above it marked by a Latin inscription telling us that it was built by Iancu de Hunedoara, Governor of the Kingdom of Hungary in 1452 (Chapter Twelve).

Much of this imposing castle is in fact older. It was given to Iancu's father Voicu by Sigismund of Luxembourg, King of Hungary (Chapter Twelve), greatly strengthened by Iancu, and added to in 1618 by Gabor Bethlen, Count of Transylvania (Chapter Twelve). Interestingly enough, there's an Orthodox church close to the castle. The Romanians were given permission to build it in 1458 by Iancu's son, whom we know as Matthias Corvinus, Hungary's outstanding king.

The Hungarians feel almost as strongly about this castle as the Serbs do about Kosovo. Without it their nation wouldn't have survived till today. When they lost Transylvania in 1919 they built a full-sized duplicate in Budapest's Town Park. In the 1950s the Romanians turned the little town of Hunedoara (pop. 7000) into a massive steel-producing centre, using ore from Transylvania's mines, and were proud that its population grew to 77,000. Pollution from the steel works grew proportionately. Not many people visit the genuine Hunyadi Castle today. It smells, and spoils the view from the castle.

An extraordinary little church at Densus, lurks in the hills half way between Roman Sarmizegetusa and Hunedoara. Densus lies west of the DN68 road from the Roman remains to Hateg. You turn off at Totesti.

The church's murals date from 1443, but no one's certain how old the rest is. The building, including its very solid roof, consists of stones taken from Roman remains, and part appears to be the mausoleum of a Roman military commander of maybe the 4th century. What's particularly unusual is that the church is topped by a slightly irregular tower made of the same enormous stone blocks.

The mountains round Brasov

After all these delights I still need to tell you about the mountain areas south and southwest of Brasov which link it with Predeal and Sinaia in Wallachia (Chapter Eleven). Together they form Romania's most-visited inland holiday region.

Poiana Brasov is Brasov's own ski and mountain resort. It's custom-built, and lies in a wonderful, sheltered hollow at the foot of Mount Postavarul, 12 km from Brasov and 1021 m above sea level. Hotels, chalets, restaurants, bars, riding centre and everything else lie well spaced out around a central lake which forms an ideal skating-rink in winter. Cable-cars take winter skiers and summer sightseers and walkers from the hollow's southern side to the Postavarul and Cristianul Mare peaks 1799 and 1690 m up.

There are chalets at the cableways' upper stations.

The ski-runs may not be spectacular, but they're sound. The winter scenery and setting are as magnificent as anyone could want. And everything is very carefully organised.

In summer it's the hollow's greenness that's specially striking, with great mountain peaks towering above it. Marked paths give you a choice of nearly a dozen walks ranging from easy to very difficult, and lasting three to twelve hours. They let you see more of the southward-stretching Bucegi Massif than is possible for ordinary holidaymakers in winter.

The Bucegi's main heights lie well south of Poiana Brasov, between the Prahova valley (Chapter Eleven) and the "Bran corridor" (below). Peaks range in height between 2000 and 2500 m on its eastern side, above the resorts of Predeal and Sinaia in the Prahova valley (Chapter Eleven). You can explore them from Poiana Brasov as well as from places in Wallachia.

The whole area has been designated a Nature Reserve, with specially protected forest areas on some of its lower slopes. In it you'll find river gorges, caves, vegetation that varies from beech and conifer forests to Alpine and sub-Alpine plants. Special reservations have also been established to protect some of the creatures found on the Bucegi – the griffon vulture, golden eagle, stag, deer, lynx, wolf, chamois, and bear, for example, though some are becoming rare today.

For ordinary visitors however the region's main delight is just its varied scenery, ranging from wild and rugged heights, to dense forest, rolling Alpine meadows, and magnificent distant views.

If you take the DN73A southwest from Brasov you come after 14 km to Risnov and the Risnov citadel (above). From here the DN73A branches east towards Predeal (Chapter Eleven). It takes you through fine scenery that includes the Postavarul and Cheisoara gorges and the pleasant minor mountain resort of Piriul Rece.

If you continue on the DN73, a further 12 km brings you to Bran Castle, perched on a low saddle directly above the road. It's shown to tourists as "Dracula's Castle", but I'm afraid this is rubbish. Bran was built at the beginning of the 13th century by a member of the Teutonic Knights, who had been settled as a colonist by King Endre (Andrew) II of Hungary. It was originally called Dietrichstein after its founder. He was driven out with the rest of his Order in 1225. In 1377 the burghers of Brasov built a new citadel here to protect their trade route with Wallachia. Vlad Tepes' ("Draculea's") only connection with Bran is that he probably attacked it around 1460 during one of many punitive raids against Brasov's Saxon traders who were using his involvement in campaigns against the Turks to cause trouble.

Regardless of any Dracula connection, Bran's a pleasantly whimsical spot. It was taken over and "romantically" altered by the Romanian royal family late last century, and became a museum in 1958. It gives you fine views into the "Bran corridor", with its mountain peaks on either side, and displays a collection of armour, weapons, furniture, and handicrafts. A small inn lies close to the castle.

South of Bran you come to what seems at first sight a simple valley. It actually runs at a considerable altitude between the massive Bucegi mountain heights to its east and the magnificently wild, sheer rock-faces of Piatra Craiului to the west.

The Piatra Craiului peaks form, in effect, an eastward continuation of the Fagaras range (above). But they combine across this "Bran corridor" to make up one of Romania's wildest and most beautiful regions. Very few people indeed lived here until new roads began to be built about 150 years ago.

Like the Bucegi, the Piatra Craiului is a Nature Reserve. You can start your walks in the region from the town of Zarnesti, 24 km from Brasov. The Plaiul Foii chalet, 12 km from the town by a pretty tough, steep path (red stripe), makes a good base for exploring an extremely lonely mountain area. There are other mountain huts within range. But you really need local advice before tackling a region like this.

Transylvanian travel

Buses criss-cross all this area. Main rail routes fan out from Brasov. One hugs the Fagaras's northern edge and makes for Arad via Sibiu, Sebes, and the Mures valley. Another turns north from Sibiu to Alba Iulia, Turda, Cluj, and Oradea. A third avoids the Fagaras and goes via Sighisoara and Alba Iulia to Arad. The main line between Bucharest and Satu Mare takes you from Brasov round the Eastern Carpathians' inner edge via Miercurea Ciuc to Dej and Baia Mare. And a cross-country line from Dej takes you over the Tihuta Pass to Suceava. The Transylvanian Depression's innermost area is served by link-lines. For air connections to Bucharest see Chapter Thirteen.

10. The Banat

The Banat forms Romania's southwestern corner. It's bounded by the Mures valley along its northern edge, by the Hungarian and Yugoslav borders on its northwest and southwest, and by the Cerna-Timis valley to the east. Apart from a few hill-slopes and the relatively small Semenic and Almaj mountain ranges, with a maximum height of 1445 m, on its eastern side, the region's very flat. It's an extension, in effect, of the Hungarian Great Plain, and like the Great Plain it's intersected by drainage canals.

It takes its name from the fact that from the late 16th century until 1718 it was occupied by Turks and ruled by a Ban, the only part of Romania apart from the coast directly ruled in this way. In 1718 it became part of Austria–Hungary and was incorporated into Romania only in 1918. Because of this period of Austro– Hungarian rule non-Romanian writers often talk about the region as though it were part of Transylvania. That's not how Romanians see it.

Visible relics of Turkish rule may not be obvious. But the memory remains. And in less obvious ways – in the region's folk music, for instance, and even in its Orthodox church chant – Turkish influence is clear.

The Mures valley

We left the Mures at Deva. It continues all the way to Arad – much longer than the 157 km the road takes – and for a very long way more across the Great Plain of Hungary before it joins the Tisa. Travelling down the valley recently I began to have visions of a canoeing trip on the Mures and on some of the other rivers in Transylvania and the Banat. Hungarian friends go canoeing a lot on the Tisa and some of its tributaries. Until at least WWI rafts were regularly used to transport goods up and down Romania's rivers. A canoe-camping trip on peaceful water through so much magnificent scenery would be wonderfully relaxing. One day?

From Deva to Arad the valley floor's flat, with trees and woods beside the river, a view of low hills to the north, and land that's largely level stretching away to the south.

At Mintia just outside Deva, close to the modern hydro-electric station and its storage lake, used for recreation by local folk, you can see remains of a major Roman settlement called Micia. Zam, 40 km on, used to be a major rafting centre. It was also once the base of a Prefect of Hunedoara County (Chapter Nine) who actually ruled the territory by day and turned highwayman at night.

Savirsin, 66 km from Deva, lies close to forests rich in game such as deer, with campsites near it. Birzava, 29 km on, makes a good starting-point for walks that aren't too demanding in the Zarand Mountains on the valley's northern side. Walkers' huts in this area stand at much lower altitudes than in, say, the Fagaras (Chapter Nine) or the Eastern Carpathians (Chapter Six) – 483 m for the Debela Gora and only 222 m for the Casoia. Note the use of "Gora" in a place-name. It's a Slav word for Mountain. In the early days of Turkish invasion Serb refugees fled northward. Their descendants still live in Romania and Hungary, and many continue their own customs. You'll find their churches there too.

Little Lipova town, 122 km from Deva, was for centuries a Turkish garrison point. It has the remains of a citadel that was once part of the Hunyadi family's possessions. What is now its Orthodox cathedral became a mosque under the Turks, and was re-consecrated after their departure. The Franciscan monastery church, built in 1756, holds a congregation of 5000.

All this is set in a very peaceful landscape today. At Soimos, however, just east of Lipova where the Mures emerges from a narrow valley there's an old fort, designed to check Tatar raids, Paulis, 14 km west of Lipova, is remembered by Romanians mainly for the ferocious fight put up by students of a local army cadets school against Nazi invaders in 1944. Siria, just outside Paulis, was the scene of some of the bitterest 1848 fighting.

But we're in a rich wine area now. If you take the side road going north you come very soon to vineyard-covered hillsides. Ghirioc, 6 km up this road, also has a walkers' hut on its outskirts which serves as a base for excursions on foot into the Zarand Mountains.

Arad remains a major communications centre despite its closeness to the modern frontiers with Hungary and Yugoslavia. The DN7 road, following the general line of the Mures, takes you westward to the frontier at Nadlac, on to Szeged in southeast Hungary, and thence into Yugoslavia. The DN69, going south from Arad, bring you to Timisoara, long the Banat's capital, after 50 km of easy driving. Northward, the DN79 takes you speedily to Chisineu-Cris, where there's another frontier crossing to Gyula and Bekescsaba in Hungary.

The main railway line from Bucharest, Cluj, Sighisoara, Alba Iulia, and Deva turns northwest at Arad to cross the Hungarian frontier at Curtici on its way to Budapest and all sorts of distant European destinations such as Prague, Berlin, Paris, and London. This is the Orient Express's route, and that of many other more recently organised international rail expresses. The town has direct air services to Bucharest, and the usual bus station.

There are several first-class hotels in the town, as well as the more modest Muresul. The Ardealul (Ardeal is Romanian for Transylvania), at 70 Bulevard Republicii, occupies a building of historical importance. In the days when it was still called the White Cross (Crucea Alba) Liszt (1846), the younger Johann Strauss (1847), Brahms (1876), and Pablo Casals (1912) gave concerts in its reception hall.

Like Cluj (Chapter Eight), Arad's most noticeable feature is the citadel on the further side of the river from the city's centre. Built in 1783 on Vauban's system, it was the work of the Austrians, and probably designed as much to keep the townsfolk in check as to guard the region. The citadel contains a monument to thirteen Hungarian revolutionary leaders executed by the Habsburgs after the confused events of the 1848 revolution

(Chapter Twelve). It's a place of annual pilgrimage for Hungarians (except when the Romanian authorities prevent them entering the country, as in 1989).

In the town centre baroque buildings predominate, giving it an atmosphere of pleasant elegance. Notable churches include a Romanian Orthodox Cathedral (Piata Filimon Sirbu) and a Serbian Orthodox Cathedral (Piata Sirbeasca), both completed in 1698, a large early 20th century Catholic church in Strada Calvin, and another older one in the citadel. Arad possesses also an old Jewish synagogue in Strada Tribunul Dobra. The suburbs have nothing to recommend them. East of the town however the Zarand Mountains' foothills are covered with vineyards and orchards full of fine peaches.

South of Arad a little promontory of Romanian soil projects into Hungary. It contains the country's most westerly town, Sinnicolau Mare. The flat land round about however lends itself well to dreary industrialised farming. It's mainly through this sort of country too that road and railway lead you southward the 51 km to Timisoara.

As the world discovered in December 1989, somewhat to its surprise, Timisoara's a decidedly elegant city, again predominantly baroque in its centre, with small parks scattered through the town, and plenty of flowers and greenery in its streets. It was originally laid out on a low hill above a gentle bend on the River Bega, now canalised, in the middle of land that was formerly swampy. A century ago Timisoara was a very go-ahead city. It introduced trams in 1869 and electric street-lighting in 1884.

Streets in the town's central area around the Piata Unirii and Piata Libertatii form a grid pattern. Everything of interest lies in this area or between it and the Bega.

Remains of the old citadel can be seen on the centre's eastern side – in Strada Popa Sapca, for instance. Its proud boast was that though repeatedly besieged it was only twice captured – by Turks in 1552 and Austrians in 1716.

The Roman Catholic Cathedral (1748) dominates Piata Unirii, with the older Serbian Orthodox Cathedral (1734) close to it in Piata Avram Iancu. The huge early twentieth century Romanian Orthodox Cathedral faces an open area in Bulevard Politehnicii. The most notable building in Piata Libertatii is the Old Town Hall. The Banat Museum in Piata Hunyadi occupies a fine 15th century Hunyadi mansion, restored at various dates in the last century and more recently.

You can see the Reformed Church where Bishop Laszlo Tokes's Hungarian congregation and their Romanian sympathisers unknowingly started Romania's recent revolution. The Opera House, opposite which the shooting finally set the popular rising in motion, stands in Piata Operei, southwest of Piata Libertatii.

Not much has changed in Timisoara since December 1989 – except people's feelings. On Christmas Day they were jubilant. During January 1990 they formulated a number of clear political demands – which have not yet been met, though they may be soon. Today they're not so certain of themselves or of their future. But Timisoara remains a lovely place to visit – as it has been for at least two centuries.

Though larger than Arad it's not a main centre for railway travel. The

DN59A road takes you west to Jimbolia and the Yugoslav frontier and the DN59 also takes you into Yugoslavia's Vojvodina Province. Railways follow the same routes. But there are not many major international expresses using these routes. The town has a good choice of first-class hotels, campsites on the outskirts, a full range of bus services, and direct flights to and from Bucharest.

The DN6, heading for Turnu Severin on the Danube, takes you after 60 km to Lugoj, another Banat town set among orchards and vineyards. You're out of the flat lands now, with the Poiana Ruscai hills to the east and the Buzias Mountains to the west. A village 35 km east has been re-named Traian Vuia in honour of the Romanian inventor who made a plane that actually flew on 18 March 1906. Vuia crashed some years later trying to fly across the Southern Carpathians, but lived to become a leading scientist and to head a group of Romanian exiles who fought in WWII with the French Resistance. He died only in 1950.

From Lugoj the DN6 continues the 42 km southeast to Caransebes, a pleasant town pleasantly placed in the middle of delightful hill, forest, and farmland scenery. A few kilometres north of Caransebes the DN58 takes you eastward to Resita, one of Romania's mountain-ringed industrial centres. The town's 68,000 inhabitants employed largely in iron and coal.

If you can't avoid going through Resita (you can also reach it direct from Lugoj by the DN58A) go as quickly as possible to Valiug, 23 km southeast. There's a hotel here, excellent mountain walking, and a cableway that takes you to the Banat Mountains' highest point, Piatra Goznei, 1445 m above the sea. This, in fact, is a

fascinating karst area. The Comarnic cave some 12 km southwest of Valiug is one of the most impressive and important in Romania. You can reach it by other side roads from Resita or from a halt on a very minor railway line.

Back on the main DN6, heading south from Caransebes, you find yourself in the extremely attractive narrow valley cut by the River Timis between the Banat's Semenic Mountains and Wallachia's Tarcu range. At Slatina Timis, 12 km from Caransebes, a minor road takes you westward to Valiug and to other places where there's good walking and, in winter, the possibility of skiing. Another 15 km or so brings you to the start of the pass dividing the valley of the Timis, which flows north, then west, then southwest and finally joins the Danube in Yugoslavia, from that of the Bela Reka (note the name: it's Slav for White River) and the streams that flow due south directly into the Danube's vast new lake beside the town of Orsova. The scenery throughout these 70-odd km is lovely. You've mountains on either side of the road and green woods at innumerable points.

A left-hand turning off the DN6 about 2 km north of your right-hand fork to Orsova brings you to the well-known spa of Baile Herculane, lying deep in the River Cerna's valley, strung out along the riverside below huge forest-covered mountain slopes. Strictly speaking, Baile Herculane belongs in my next chapter. But it's more convenient to mention it here.

Baile Herculane is one of Romania's most famous spas. It was used by people such as the Austrian rulers Empress Maria Theresa and Emperor Franz Jozef II, as well as innumerable notable Romanians. I'm not qualified to judge spas' medical qualities – one reason why I've mentioned only a very few of the large number found in Romania. But Baile Herculane has the sort of setting that would improve anyone's health. To crown everything the Mehedinti Mountains behind the spa contain the large Domogled Nature Reserve, described by specialist writers as home to "one of the richest floras in Europe, with numerous Mediterranean and endemic species". Plants found here include a great variety of oaks, Banat pine, Turkish hazel, Eastern hornbeam, and an undergrowth of lilac, juniper, and much else set among beech and sycamore and maple.

You've half-a-dozen hotels to choose from at Baile Herculane.

Orsova's about 20 km from Baile Herculane. It stands on the shore of what was once part of the Danube's most turbulent section and is now a vast, placid storage lake stretching 100 km or more upstream. The lake was created by the huge Yugoslav–Romanian barrage across the Danube inaugurated in September 1964. I start my next chapter's journey at the dam.

The barrage raised the water level some 20 m – far above the old town of Orsova. A new, grid-pattern town now stands on the slopes above the lake, and a new road, not yet wholly complete, now follows the lake's new contours 100 km or so to another new version of what was a new town centuries ago. This is Moldova Noua, New Moldavia, settled originally by Moldavian refugees.

The lake's scenery is spectacular, both on its Romanian and its Yugoslav side. It's where the mighty Danube has cut a spectacular gorge through high mountains. The views down into the man-made lake are magnificent from the mountain heights on both its sides.

The new lake and barrage provide Romania and Yugoslavia with 10 billion KW of power each, as well as making navigation upstream as well as down simple and stress-free. On this stretch of the river the most powerful tugs could once manage an upstream speed of no more then 2–3 knots, and the channel was far too narrow to make the passages simple. Now the lake speeds commercial traffic and provides the perfect setting for water sports and holidays. Or rather, it would if any of the essential infrastructure and facilities had been built. Alas, they haven't.

11. Wallachia's Mountains and Plain

Wallachia means "country of the Wallachs" or Vlachs, as the nomadic Wallach shepherds who wandered through parts of modern Yugoslavia were called. As a student reading classics I was told these Vlachs spoke almost pure Latin. No one seemed then to realise that it was ordinary Romanian.

But Wallachia was in times past often also called Muntenia, "Land of Mountains", which seems odd since the Danube (Dunarea in Romanian) has always been its natural southern frontier and there's a considerable stretch of flat plain between Southern Carpathians and Danube.

Even today it's sometimes divided into Muntenia, "Land of Mountains" and Oltenia, "Land of the River Olt", which again seems odd, and not only because it seemingly turns a blind eye to the plain. The WWII administrative areas fixed by the Nazi invaders, which continued unchanged until the later 1960s, included a sizable unit called "Oltenia". But it took in only a tiny length of the lower Olt River.

With all this in mind I shall start this chapter on the Danube where we ended the previous chapter, close to what was once the frightening Iron Gates gorge. From there I'll take you to Tirgu Jiu and up the Jiu to the Retezat Nature Reserve and the Paring Mountains. From Tirgu Jiu we'll go eastwards across the Carpathian foothills to Rimnicu Vilcea

and up the River Olt's magnificent long gorge to Sibiu (Chapter Nine).

Next we'll tackle what has always been called "the Arges" – the mountain area round the Arges river which rises in the Southern Carpathians and flows southwards to the Danube plain and into the Danube, parallel with Jiu and Olt. After that we'll look at the River Prahova's valley cutting through the Southern Carpathians parallel with the Arges, Olt and Jiu and carrying road and railway from Bucharest to Brasov, and at other lovely mountain roads between these two major cities. And finally we'll think about the huge Danube and the plain which, with the Banat, covers a third of all Romania's territory. All of this goes to make up Wallachia's ancient principality.

When travelling in this part of Romania it's important to realise that the Carpathian horseshoe's heights continue untamed in an almost straight southwesterly line till they clash with the even more powerful Danube and are cut in two by it. You can find some of the country's loveliest, wildest, loneliest mountain expanses within a 120 km radius of the Iron Gates gorge. In ancient days the Dacians used these mountains as a sort of fortifying wall. Today they're valued mainly for their minerals.

The Iron Gates

If you want to understand the terrors

Cap Aurora is one of Romania's modern Black Sea resorts.

Countryfolk still buy at the annual
Maidens' Fair mountaintop gathering
in Transylvania.

Peleş, at Sinaia in Wallachia's Prahova valley, was built as a royal palace for Romania's first King in 1883.

Over 1400 steps form part of the steep path leading to the medieval ruins of Poienari Castle in Wallachia's Argeş region

of the Danube's Iron Gates you need to look at old photographs and old guidebooks such as the Admiralty's excellent River Danube handbook published in 1920 (the Danube was an international waterway and the Admiralty felt obliged to produce something equivalent to another of their world-famous charts). The vast sea-like Danube, just at the point where the modern DN67 comes close to the river after the DN57 has forked west to Orsova, was squeezed into a wildly turbulent 25 m wide channel, aptly called (in Romanian) *Cazanele*, the Cauldrons. It all looks magnificently peaceful today.

About 8 km downstream the mountains on either side of the Danube suddenly give way to flat land and you see the huge Iron Gates hydro-electric barrage stretching right across the river. It's 448 m long and 30 m high, with locks big enough for the river's largest freighters and barges, and turbines that provide 20 billion KW of electricity. It also acts as a bridge, carrying a road that makes an important link between Romania and Yugoslavia.

People who've never seen the Danube don't realise what a barrier to easy communication its last 2000 km between Vienna and the sea beyond its Black Sea Delta have been till very recent years. Not only is the river's main channel enormously wide. It used also to flood regularly to a width of 30 or 40 kilometres till containing dykes were built in the 19th century.

No bridge crossed it below Vienna till the beautiful Szechenyi "Chain Bridge", beloved of all Budapest's citizens, was thrown across it in 1842. Even today the only roadways crossing the river below Budapest are at Novi Sad, Belgrade, and Smederevo in Yugoslavia, and at the Iron Gates, Giurgiu (below), and Giurgeni (Chapter Five) in Romania.

The nearest town to the dam on the Romanian side is Turnu Severin, which the Romanians like to call Drobeta-Turnu Severin because of the Roman town that once stood there. It's an oddly modern-looking, grid-pattern town, and was in fact laid out only in 1833. Five years earlier the sizable village of Cerneti, 6 km downstream, had been destroyed by Turks. The inhabitants were given permission to resettle at Turnu Severin. Within twenty years modern navigation had begun on the Danube with the building of dykes and the buoying of navigation channels. By 1851 Turnu Severin had a port and by 1858 a shipbuilding yard. Both were totally destroyed in WWII, but have been rebuilt and greatly enlarged.

But for the ordinary visitor the town's main interest lies in its Roman remains. Here you can see remains of the remarkable Roman bridge, 1350 m long, 13.50 wide, and 18.60 m above the water level, built for the Emperor Trajan of Damascus in AD 103–105. Parts of the bridge's northern end and one of the twenty pillars that supported it have survived. The remains can be seen a little downstream from the riverside jetty reached from the Bulevard Dunarea (Danube) in the town's centre.

Remains of extensive Roman baths stand on the bridge's upstream side, suggesting that Roman troops and travellers were glad to relax in the sauna heat and enjoy an invigorating cold dip after the long march north. But perhaps it was just a convenient site for soldiers guarding the bridgehead from the fort whose remains lie just beyond the little 13th century Orthodox church in the garden round a school called after Trajan (who else?) close to the bridge's end.

The Iron Gates (*Portile de Fier*) Museum, a little further inland still from the church (in Strada Independentei), contains a good exhibition explaining the region's history and importance. The whole of Cazanele, the Cauldrons, is today protected as a Nature Reserve because of its botanical as well as historical value.

The jetty where the large Danube cruise vessels call stands opposite the town's centre, with the railway station nearby, and the bus terminal and Hotel Traian also close. The newer Hotel Parc lies a fair way from the river, in Bulevard Vladimirescu, with the campsite still further inland, reached along Strada Crisan.

Before you leave Turnu Severin you may like to make a 30 km excursion into the Mehedinti hills by a side road that leads northwest off the DN67 just outside the town. It takes you into the hills above the Topolnita valley to the village of Ciresu and Pestera Topolnita (Topolnita Cave), the longest and most important of all Romania's karst caverns. The cave's quite close to the Bahna fossil reserve. But to reach that you need to take the train to Virciorova halt, some 17 km west of Turnu Severin and 5 km west of the Iron Gates' narrowest point, and walk up the rough track to Illovita village (about an hour). Here you can also visit the remains of Vodnita Monastery and church, built in the 14th century and destroyed by the Turks in 1524 but never restored. Two further hours bring you to the fossil reserve.

Tirgu Jiu and the Retezat

From Turnu Severin the DN67 leads inland, northeastward and directly away from the Danube, to Motru (35 km) and Tirgu Jiu (84 km). It's a run over mainly flat land, parallel with the Carpathian foothills, crossing innumerable small streams flowing southeast to the Danube.

Tirgu Jiu, like most of Romania's "market" (Tirgu) towns, stands at the point where the river it's named after emerges from the hills. It's not a very attractive town, though the Old Town Hall (Primaria Veche: erected in 1898) and the Cathedral (1764), both in Piata Victoriei, are worth seeing. Ecaterina Teodoroiu's mausoleum faces the Town Hall. She was an extraordinary young woman, aged twenty in 1914, who somehow contrived to join the Romanian army, was given a commission, and died leading her detachment into battle in 1917. The house where she was born has been turned into a small museum (in Bulevard 1 Mai, close to the Old Town Hall).

The real reason for stopping off in Tirgu Jiu – and it's a very good one – is to see the Brancusi sculptures. Brancusi is only half-remembered in the West today. But before WWII he was called "the father of modern sculpture". In the park down by the River Jiu you'll find the Table of Silence, the Avenue of Chairs, and the Gateway of the Kiss. The photographs of them that you see in some art books give you no idea of the impact they make in their proper setting, perhaps because their masses are related to traditional carved wooden objects that belong in this region (Brancusi was born in the village of Hobnita, 25 km from Tirgu Jiu). I find looking at them in their proper setting a very moving experience.

Brancusi had intended that the ensemble in the gardens should be linked with the Column of Endless Memory (to give it its proper name: it's usually inaccurately called the Endless Column) and the Festive Table on a slight eminence well to the east. The column of Endless Memory, a 30 m high geometrical copper-coated pig-iron structure recalling the Pillar of Heaven in Romanian folk tales and intended as a memorial to the dead of WWI, was placed where he'd intended with the Festive Table close to it.

The linking sculptures were never added. And today, if you try to follow the linking line that Brancusi had in mind, you'll find you have to clamber across a bunch of railway lines and maybe through or under some goods waggons. Even so, I'm still prepared to make a special trip to Tirgu Jiu to look at Brancusi's work.

When I first saw the column, I was told that in 1948 some bright proletarian revolutionaries had decided this decadent nonsense ought to be pulled down. So they attached a steel hawser to the column and looped its further end round a large tractor's suspension. They drove the tractor away – fast – and lost half their machine. Surprise, surprise! Why do so many people imagine artists must by definition be unpractical asses? To make a 100-foot-high pig iron column stand securely upright by itself requires a fair amount of practical ability. The best joiner I've ever known was a girl sculptor who worked in wood.

Tirgu Jiu's not only the Gorj county town. It's also a major communications and industrial centre. I've enjoyed staying at its main hotel, the Gorjul, in Strada Eroilor. It has a campsite too.

One interesting excursion takes you westward the 44 km to Baia de Arama on the road numbered 67D, with several useful stops on the way.

At Birsesti, 4 km from Tirgu Jiu, you can turn off north to the villages of Stanesti and Valari to see the Susitei gorges and waterfall. At 13.5 km from Tirgu Jiu you can make another diversion north to Runcu village and the wild scenery of the Runcu Gorges. From Pestisani, 22 km from Tirgu Jiu you can turn off yet again, southward this time, to reach Hobita, Brancusi's native village (his birthplace, naturally, is a museum).

At Tismana, which has a major fete on 15 August, the Feast of the Assumption, and also a campsite, you can turn north once more to reach Tismana Monastery and the Tismana Gorge and caves. Standing over 500 m above sea level the monastery was built in the 14th century, enlarged at various dates, and then very well fortified in 1633–34. It's considered among the most beautiful of all Romania's fortified monasteries. From Tismana too a local road takes you to Topesti and the Gura Plaiului cave.

There's a further, even more spectacular limestone cavern at Closani, 12 km off the DN67D on a side road 9 km beyond Tismana. And if you continue the 4 km to Baia de Arama you can make a final diversion – southward – to the natural bridge and limestone caves at Ponoare. You may be involved in a fair amount of scrambling here.

A road has been planned that will continue from Baia de Arama, a mining centre whose copper was exhausted two centuries ago, across the hills, down the Cerna valley, and through the Cerna Gorge to Baile Herculane. But it's not yet complete.

From Tirgu Jiu however your main destination is likely to be a trip northward up the DN66 to Petrosani, the Vilcan, Paring, and Retezat Mountains and the Retezat Nature Reserve, biggest, wildest, and most spectacular of all Romania's protected areas.

The scenery's lovely throughout this journey. The River Jiu has cut a deep gorge between the Paring Mountains to the east, with their highest peak, Paringul Mare, the Great Paring, standing at 2518 m, and the Vilcan Mountains, which reach 1870 m, to the west. Much of the valley's forested, and villages infrequent.

Just 11 km from Tirgu Jiu a road forking east takes you to the village of Curtisoara, where you can see a *cula* (semi-fortified tower house of the type widely found in Romania). It houses a small handicraft museum.

Another 8 km and we're starting the climb up the wild and picturesque Lainici Pass. It's another 15 km before we're on the pass's northern side, at Livezeni, only 5 km short of Petrosani.

Here a well-surfaced road runs westward to Vulcan, Lupeni, and Uricani, all today major coal-mining and industrial centres. They're also however the starting-points for trips into some of Romania's wildest and most striking mountain areas.

The Retezat massif, on the road's northern side, covers some 750 sq km. Its highest peaks, the Pealeaga, Papusa, Retezat, and Virful Mare (the Great Peak) are all just above or below 2500 m. But there are twenty that top 2300 m and forty over 2200 m. Glacial cirques, where the snow continues till July, add a spectacular setting to the grandiose chaos of the mountain peaks' tumbled, jagged rocks. Peaceful glacial lakes – 82 in all – mirror crags and sky. The largest, Bucura, covers some 11 ha. Several others have areas of over 3 ha. Apart from the glaciers that once filled the cirques the locations of eighteen others have been identified. They were longer and larger than any glaciers that ever existed elsewhere in Romania.

The region's fauna and flora are superb. Stags have almost disappeared because of the wolves. But wild boar are numerous and bears thrive. The lynx has found a good home here, and chamois flourish in the heights, away from tourists.

Lammergeyers from Bulgaria or Yugoslavia sometimes still appear here, though the last native bird was shot in 1894. The golden eagle, the griffon vulture (*gyps fulvus*), the black vulture (*aegypius monachus*), and a host of other fascinating birds live and breed here. But even all that's only a beginning. The Retezat National Park covers some 10,000 ha, of which 2000 form a scientific reserve where hunting, fishing, grazing and forestry are forbidden.

There are enough huts and marked paths to make full exploration on foot of all three mountain ranges possible. But you'd be well advised to ask about the latest regulations before you plan a journey there. The Romanian National Tourist Offices in London, New York, and elsewhere should be able to help – but do ask in plenty of time. For on-the-spot sightseeing trips consult the Tourist Information Offices in Tirgu Jiu or Lupeni (both in streets named after Tudor Vladimirescu) or at the one in Petrosani (87 Strada Republicii).

From Petrosani, a not very prepossessing coal-mining town

(though it has a useful, sizable hotel), a new road is being driven eastward between the Lotru and Capatini Mountains, which will intersect another new road running all the way from Sebes to the DN67 east of Tirgu Jiu in a particularly lonely mountain area. If you continue north from Petrosani on the DN66 you come after another 54 km of mostly lovely scenery to Hateg (Chapter Nine), with the Sebes Mountains and the ancient Dacian strongholds (Chapter Nine) to your east.

Rimnicu Vilcea and the Olt Valley

The DN67 running east from Tirgu Jiu, offers rather quieter views on its way to Rimnicu Vilcea, 113 km distant. You've the by now familiar views of Carpathian foothills to the north and flat Danube plain to the south. The main points of interest are a group of monasteries roughly half way between the two towns.

About 50 km from Tirgu Jiu a road on your left takes you the 5 km to Baja de Fier, where there are graphite mines, and a further 3 km to the Muerii Cave, with more striking limestone formations. From here you can cut across directly to Polovragi village with its many houses typical of this region and Polovragi Monastery on its outskirts. It was completed and decorated by Constantin Brincoveanu himself (Chapter Twelve) in the early 18th century. The frescos in the monastery's infirmary are particularly fine. A kilometre from the monastery the Polovragi Cave in the Oltetul (Little Olt) Gorge is a typical limestone cavern, and the narrow, deep Oltetul Gorge, 2 km long, is a wild and colourful spot.

From Polovragi you can drive directly east to Hurezu Monastery, thought by many to be possibly the most beautiful in all Romania – which is saying quite a lot. Its particular joy is its highly decorative Brincovenesc architecture (Chapter Twelve). The church's fine frescos, its richly decorated iconostasis, and its massive carved pearwood doors are also remarkable. The monastery was founded and built by Constantin Brincoveanu himself, with the support of his whole family. Buildings round the church include a residence for the prince. The original work was completed in 1697. The belfry was added in 1753. The monastery's name appears sometimes as Hurez and sometimes Hurezi as well as Hurezu. But the town nearby seems always to be Horezu.

Some of my Romanian friends in bygone days used to make special trips to Hurezu Monastery for a reason quite unconnected with its architecture. They went to hear one of its monks beating the *toaca*. In many Orthodox regions (not only Romania) hammering on metal or wood is used where Western churches for preference use bells. In its most elaborate form the Romanian *toaca* is beaten on a suspended beechwood plank by a man or woman using two beechwood mallets.

Certain rhythms are compulsory – you'll sometimes hear these tapped out in a very simple way by someone carrying a plank and using a single hammer. But the best performers cover the obligatory figures with decorative devices that would be a credit to the best jazz drummers – who don't have to tap on alternate spots with one hand and continuously repeat the sign of the cross with the other, as Romanian monks and nuns do.

The first *toaca* I ever heard was at Putna (Chapter Six) on New Year's Eve at the start of the St Basil's Day (1 January) watchnight service. Hearing the rhythmic hammering ringing out across the darkened mountains is something I'll never forget. Happily I was able to record most of the performance for a BBC-radio programme I was preparing. My spine still tingles when I play it.

Near Costesti village, about 6 km east of Horezu town, you'll find two further monasteries of considerable interest – Bistrita and Arnota. The original Bistrita was destroyed by artillery fire in 1509, but rebuilt and heavily fortified at various periods since then. A cave near the monastery contains two small churches that formed part of a hermitage. It's also a favourite spot for bats. Striking scenery round the monastery includes the Bistrita Gorges. Arnota was built in 1633 and restored by Prince Constantin Brincoveanu.

Maldaresti, 4 km south of Horezu town, contains two fortified homes of the type called *cula*. They date from the 18th and 19th centuries. One houses a folk museum.

You reach a turning on the right 26 km from Horezu which leads to Baile Govora, one of Romania's small spas set in fine scenery. From here you can visit two more beautifully-sited monasteries and a specially fascinating small wooden church. You'll probably have to walk the 4 km or so.

Govora Monastery dates from 1496. Surpatele nearby was another Brincoveanu foundation. The little monastery church near it is famous as "biserica dintr' o lemn", the church from a single tree-trunk. It has been rebuilt on a stone footing. But legend says it was really constructed

originally from a single oak-tree.

Back on the DN67 it's only 10 km or so to Vilcea's county town. Rimnicu Vilcea. With two sound hotels and a nearby campsite it's a useful stopping-place before you set off up the Olt's remarkable long, steep valley to Sibiu (Chapter Nine). If you're as nuts about Romanian traditional music as I am (and if you've any interest whatever in music you ought to be) you'll stay long enough to see the little museum housed in Anton Pann's home.

He was an Orthodox priest who lived from 1797 to 1854 and was one of the world's earliest collectors of folk music. We owe him an enormous debt for having preserved a considerable number of magnificent tunes, including one of Romania's loveliest Christmas carols. *Trei crai de la rasarit* (Three kings from the east). Romania has hundreds of very lovely Christmas carols. But virtually none have been heard in Britain apart from the well-known *O ce veste minunata* (Oh, what wonderful good tidings) played to the crowds in Timisoara on Christmas Day 1989 by Radio Timisoara and relayed to us. None of our commentators noticed the irony of the words.

The 100 km from Rimnicu Vilcea to Sibiu on the DN7 are pure joy the whole way. Until you begin to emerge from the Olt gorge at Talmaciu, about 25 km from Sibiu, you're driving almost continuously in a deep, narrow valley beside the rapidly-flowing river, sparkling in the sun, alongside steep mountain slopes clothed in thick, dark green forests. It's the sort of enormously impressive drive you hope will never end. And there's a lot to see along the road.

The first major settlement you come to is Calimanesti spa, 16 km from

Rimnicu Vilcea. Its hotels and houses are strung out along the valley floor, very much as at Baile Herculane (above). A small bridge across the river leads to Jiblea, built over the remains of the Roman camp which guarded this vital road. An island in the river has been laid out as a park. It includes a hermitage built in 1522.

Calimanesti's northern edge includes the hamlet of Caciulata, and the spa is sometimes called Calimanesti-Caciulata. Almost as soon as the buildings end you come to Cozia Monastery, neatly filling flat land between river and road (the railway's on the valley's further side at this point). It looks very sheltered between its high mountain walls. But the altitude here is actually 300 m. Winter can be chilly.

Cozia was built by Prince Mircea the Old (Chapter Twelve) in 1388. The church's open porch was added by Prince Constantin Brincoveanu. Frescos inside the church were painted from the 14th century on. Those on the outside walls, not nearly as striking as those you've seen on the exteriors of Moldavia's "Painted Churches" (Chapter Six), but still very attractive, date from the 18th century. Mircea's buried in the church. Cozia's a wonderful spot for a restful stop. You can look straight down into the river from the edge of the monastery's boundary.

There are other monasteries near Cozia – Turnu and Stinisoara, both on the mountain slopes below Mount Cozia's summit (1677 m) east of the river. But the main interest of this part of the valley is the Nature Reserve on Mount Cozia and the valley's scenery. The Nature Reserve contains Alpine plants, and a hut close to the summit provides a base for walkers.

Down in the valley the Olt runs through a white water stretch, with bends known as Cirligul Mare and Cirligul Mic (Big Hook and Little Hook) and Armasarul (The Stallion). In bygone days they caused men steering freight rafts many problems. Mount Naratu, facing Mount Cozia across the gorge, surveys the scene from its western side.

You come to the gorge's only real road junction 30 km north of Rimnicu Vilcea. The road joining from the west is part of the new route running east from Petrosani, which I mentioned earlier in this chapter. It follows the River Lotru, flowing between the Lotru and Capatini Mountains, and leads to mountain resorts, such as Voineasa, in charming settings but still being developed.

At Ciineni, 50 km from Pitesti, we come to another particularly narrow valley section, which lasts almost until we reach the flatter plateau south of Sibiul. The Valea Oltului chalet and restaurant some 14 km beyond Ciineni make another useful halting-place. The defile ends at Turnu Rosu (Red Tower), the remains of a 15th century fort.

One thing that needs to be pointed out about this lovely mountain valley is that the Olt, which created it, flows steadily south the whole way. In the course of millions of years it has cut for itself this escape route out of the area inside the Carpathian horseshoe, after already flowing a very long way – first south past Miercurea Ciuc, then north near Brasov, later west along the Fagaras's northern edge, before finally turning south near Sibiu. Even at Rimnicu Vilcea it still has nearly 150 km to go – much more if you count all its bends – before it reaches the Danube.

The railway's route through the Olt valley is every bit as picturesque as the road's. In some ways, in fact, it's perhaps more attractive because the line crosses the river several times and is often buried down on the valley floor. Buses operate between Rimnicu Vilcea and Sibiu too.

The Arges

The River Arges flows north-south roughly parallel with the Olt, some 50 km to its east. But unlike the Olt the Arges rises high on the Fagaras ridge. To use its valley to reach the Brasov-Sibiu road (Chapter Nine) you have to cross the saddle above Lake Bilea between Romania's highest mountains, Mount Negoiu to the west (2535 m) and Moldoveanu to the east (2543 m) (Chapter Nine). I propose to take you northward up the Arges.

Your effective starting-point is the little town of Curtea de Arges – Arges Palace, one of Wallachia's ancient capitals. You can reach it by a recently-constructed road, the DN73C, which turns northeast off the DN7 some 12 km southeast of Rimnicu Vilcea. The town stands 450 m above the sea on flat land where the river valley widens.

The first spot everyone flocks to in Curtea de Arges is the staggering, vast Monastery Church. It's covered outside with stone carved in amazingly intricate and beautiful patterns. They continue right to the tops of its towers, two of which have long window-slits designed to make them look as though they've been twisted in opposite directions. Close-up, the doorway appears to be an enormous piece of stone lace.

The church was completed in 1526. Its founder was Prince Neagoe Basarab, and it's linked to one of the best-known of all Romanian legends, that of Master Manole, the architect-builder. Mestru Manole's the subject of an epic ballad that appears in many forms. But the essence of the story is that the builder first had to immure his wife in the walls and then to kill himself (in case he produced a building to rival this) by throwing himself from the top of the church. A spring appeared at the spot where he fell – and to prove it's all true you'll be shown the spring.

Monastery buildings surround the church. Elegant though they are, they don't in any way compete with the central building.

The other part of Curtea de Arges which draws visitors is the remains of the old palace itself. Over 100 m long and nearly 80 wide (not a regular rectangle), it was tremendously strongly fortified with thick walls built from boulders taken from the River Arges. The palace's small church, Sfintu Nicolae Domnesc, dates from around 1320, but has been altered and restored many times since then. The last restoration, completed in 1920, attempted to give the church its original appearance.

There's a sound hotel at Curtea de Arges, but it's obviously one of the stopping-places that can be filled with coach tourists in the high summer season. The campsite on the outskirts of Curtea de Arges is also apt to be busy at peak holiday periods.

At Corbeni, 18 km north of Curtea de Arges on the DN7C, you can see another two-storeyed fortified *cula*. There's a restaurant and campsite near it, as well as a small hotel.

A further 10 km or so brings you to a remarkable conical hill directly west of the road, which is topped by remains of a castle. It's the citadel known as

Poenari or Poienari. Ancient documents suggest that it was built by Vald Tepes ("Draculea") in the 15th century, and that it was here that he forced rebellious boyars to carry stones up the hillside for long periods till they dropped dead. Excavations suggest the buildings are older.

What is certain is that Poienari fits very nearly perfectly the description of Dracula's castle given by Bram Stoker, though he locates it in Szekler country near Bistrita (Chapter Eight). Its ruins have been partially restored. But to reach it you have to climb an extraordinarily steep path, rebuilt some years ago to incorporate over 1400 steps. At the top it's not quite true that a stone dropped from a window would fall a thousand feet (if there were any windows). But you can easily throw a stone clear of the ruined walls and have it drop several hundred feet before it hits anything. To prevent accidents and suicides wire netting has had to be stretched on firm supports around the whole fortress. It's a very spectacular spot, but you need to be fit to reach it.

The modern Vidraru hydro-electric dam starts just beyond Poienari. A forestry road makes a complete circuit of the 14-km-long storage lake possible and provides magnificent views. From here the road winds on over the pass to Lake Bilea and Arpasu de Jos on the DN7 between Brasov and Sibiu (Chapter Nine).

From Bucharest to Brasov

We're back in Bucharest now, where we started this journey round Romania. You can reach Brasov from here only by one railway line, but there's a variety of roads that are all outstandingly attractive and interesting in different ways.

The most direct and most used is the route up the River Prahova valley to its summit at Predeal, then down into Brasov. You'll certainly want to travel this way before you try out the other, longer roads. But these other roads also have a lot that's interesting and no shortage of fine views.

To see the Prahova valley you first drive (or take the train) the 60 km to Ploiesti. Bypass roads enable you to avoid Ploiesti's centre. Apart from the Paralela 45 restaurant and campsite at Kilometre 80 (from Bucharest, 20 from Ploiesti) the first main settlement you notice is Cimpina, 37 km from Ploiesti. We're still in oil country, but this spot's main attraction is the former prison of Doftana (or Dofteana), on a hilltop 4 km northeast of the town.

Doftana was notorious for its torture and murders in fascist days and has been preserved as a museum. Cimpina has a small hotel, and a museum devoted to the painter Nicolae Grigorescu, who began his career as an artist at Agapia Monastery (Chapter Six).

Comarnic, 32 km further along the road, has a useful campsite and restaurant. It's only 14 km from the lovely tourist centre of Sinaia. The town takes its name from a small monastery whose church contains a stone carried all the way many centuries ago from remote and (in those days) almost inaccessible St Catherine's monastery in the Sinai Desert. It was chosen as the site for the first king of Romania's summer palace in 1875. And because it lies almost 800 m up at the foot of the wild Bucegi massif it has become important as a skiing centre in winter and a base for mountain excursions in summer.

It was the monastery that caused the originally tiny settlement to change its name in 1878, when the railway was built through the valley – from Izvorul (The Spring) to the more imposing Sinaia. The tiny monastery church dates from 1695 and deserves at least a quick visit.

Peles Castle, the former royal residence, was completed in 1883. It's an imposing building, displaying a fine eclectic choice of architectural styles – English and Italian renaissance, baroque, rococo, and Hispano-Moorish, with German renaissance predominant. It sounds terrible, but the results in fact are surprisingly pleasing. You can visit its ceremonial hall, the hall of mirrors, the armoury containing Turkish equipment captured in 1877–78 along with older weapons, the Hall of Pillars, guest rooms, and a lot more. Most of the original furniture is still in place. Terraces on each side of the palace are laid out like an amphitheatre, with an English-style garden. They make a fine setting.

Foisor, the palace's 40-roomed hunting lodge, stands close by. Pelisor, the "little palace", built between 1899 and 1903, was intended for the heir to the throne and is now a writers' home.

Sinaia's well-placed as a centre for both winter and summer holidays. The slopes of the Bucegi Masif (Chapter Nine) rise steeply west of the town, continuing to a whole series of peaks well over 200 m. The ski runs' altitudes vary between 1000 and 2000 m. Five excellent hotels are spread out along the main road and one, the Alpin, stands at the first cable-car's upper station at Cota 1400, 600 m above the station and 1400 above the sea. Villa accommodation is also available.

A second cable-car, with a chair-lift roughly parallel with it continues from Cota 1400 to Cota 2000, where there's another hotel. Chairlifts serve a number of other points, ski-tows are available on the slopes, and there's a full complement of strategically-located chalets with restaurants and bars.

The ski-runs themselves are not perhaps likely to attract experts in great numbers. But they're popular with ordinary skiers. One 8-km track, from the Miorita cabin to the Babele also has been laid out for cross-country enthusiasts. A 1500-m bobsleigh track with a fall of 300 m winds down from the Hotel Alpin towards the valley.

In summer, marked paths – or the cableways – take you up to the chalets and beyond them into the high mountains. They aren't recommended for any but really experienced mountain folk in winter.

Busteni, a further 8 km up the valley, provides another good base for summer walking, and in winter acts as a sort of link between Sinaia and the Prahova valley's other main ski resort, Predeal.

At Predeal the ski-slopes lie on the valley's further side, and the resort's installations are rather simpler. A twin chair-lift takes you from Clabucet-Sosire (Clabucet-Arrival) on the lower slopes (1050 m) to the Clabucet-Plecare (Clabucet-Departure) chalet (1456 m), where the two runs graded "difficult" begin. There's a fair variety of easy slopes, one rather limited beginners' area, and a 2.5 km cross-country run. A second cross-country piste is available on the hills to the west.

Hotels, scattered through the town and close to ski slopes, are more numerous than at Sinaia.

Three western alternatives to this Prahova valley route between Bucharest and Brasov start at Pitesti or Tirgoviste. The DN71 runs from Tirgoviste to Sinaia. The DN73 takes you from Pitesti to Brasov via Cimpulung. The DN72A from Tirgoviste joins the DN73 at Dragoslavele and continues through the Giuvala Pass to Bran Castle (Chapter Nine).

Tirgoviste's a worthwhile tourist destination in its own right. The town itself is messy. But the remains of the former Princely Court are tremendously impressive, though you'll really need a knowledgable guide to explain all the excavations to you. Wallachia's capital was moved here from Curtea de Arges early in the 15th century, in the days when the first Turkish attacks were having to be beaten off.

The palace's church of the Assumption (Adormirea Maicii Domnului), also called Great Palace Church (Domneasca Mare), and the Holy Friday church (Sfintu Veneri), known too as Little Palace Church (Domneasca Mica), remain renovated and intact. The former boasts fine frescos. The impressive 15th century Chindia (Sunset) tower, part of the palace defences, was destroyed by an earthquake in 1802 but subsequently rebuilt.

If you're bound for Brasov, the DN71, running almost due north from Tirgoviste, takes you up onto a sort of high plateau that forms a peaceful lower southward extension of the wild Bucegi Mountains above Sinaia and Predeal, and drops you into the Prahova valley just south of Sinaia.

The second road starts from Pitesti, an oil town second only to Ploiesti in importance, whose situation at the

edge of the Danube Plain it very much resembles.

You reach Pitesti from Bucharest along Romania's only stretch of genuine motorway (A1). Though it doesn't look an attractive town as you approach, its old centre contains some fine buildings, not only the Princely Church from 1656 in Strada Doamna Balasa and the former County Hall (1898–89) that now houses the County Museum (Strada Horea, Closca, si Crisan – what an address!), but also some modern shopping complexes.

From Pitesti you take the DN73 northeast to Cimpulung, Wallachia's first capital. The church of the Negru Voda monastery, founded by Wallachia's first ruler, Prince Basarab I, in the early 14th century, is its main attraction. The 14th century Catholic church in Strada Negru Voda contains a gravestone inscribed with the name Laurentiu de Longo Campo and the date 1300. It's the first documentary mention of the town under the name Cimpulung (= Longo Campo). There are other relics of the original palace area.

The main appeal of this area however is simply the atmosphere of greenness and peace. As you go north you come after 42 km to the Giuvala Pass, the real boundary between ancient Wallachia and ancient Transylvania, though the burghers of Brasov found it convenient to build their customs point on the Bran saddle. From the Giuvala to Bran the road runs through the Bran corridor (Chapter Nine).

The DN72A starts eastward, then turns northeast up the Dimbovita valley for some 64 km. It, too, takes you up into a pleasant green countryside, with Mount Leaota (2134 m) east of you. Despite the mountain's height you don't feel that you're really in mountain country.

There's a fourth alternative road to Brasov from Bucharest. It follows the DN1A from Ploiesti up the Teleajen's valley and over the Bratocea Pass east of the Prahova valley and the DN1. It's the route used regularly before the DN1 was built in the 19th century. If you take the DN1A from Bucharest to Ploiesti you'll find the distance is 71 km instead of 60. But you get a chance to stop off at Mogosoia and see Brincoveanu's palace (Chapter Four) as you start your trip. The total distance from Bucharest by DN1A works out at 185 km instead of the DN1's 166.

The main interest along this route is the Slanic Salt Mountain (Muntele de Sare), where salt has been mined since the 17th century from a bed that was 6 km long, 3 km wide, and 600 m thick. It's a Nature Reserve today. You can visit the ancient workings and see the lake and the extraordinarily colourful formations round it created by the collapse of an early mineshaft. A legend recounts that a bride deserted on her wedding day threw herself off a nearby mountain peak into the abyss below, creating the sparkling lake, and giving it its name of Lacul al Miresei, the Bride's Lake.

The Muntele de Sare lies a little off the DN1A, and a new road to Slanic has been built in recent years which forks right from the DN1 northwest of Ploiesti. You have to look out for the signs – though the road's well used by excursion coaches in summer. There's a campsite near Slanic, and you can rejoin the DN1A beyond the town.

Maneciu's the last main settlement before you begin the climb to the Bratocea Pass's summit. It's also the furthest point reached by the railway serving this area.

The mountain scenery becomes even more attractive as the road climbs. About 13 km from here a side road on your left leads to the Suzana Monastery, founded in 1740, with its present church built a century later. Like Agapia (Chapter Six), Suzana's used as a holiday centre by Romanians who rent simple accommodation in the nuns' cottages. It's a blissful, peaceful spot – unless you happen to have noisy children, or similar folk, as your holidaymaking neighbours.

Cheia's the nearest village on the DN1A. It's the base for a number of fine walks, most of them not too strenuous though some are fairly long, on the slopes of the Ciucas Mountains. The destinations are the Muntele Rosu chalet, at 1260 m, the Gropsoarele-Zaganul peak (1860 m), the Ciucas chalet (1550 m), and Mount Ciucas's summit (1959).

The Danube Plain

Considering the size of the Danube Plain, it seems churlish to describe it as of little interest. Geographers and farmers may not see it as miles of damn-all, but that's how it appears to tourists – however interested they may be in the life and customs of the people who live and work on it.

Its largest town, with a population over 250,000, is Craiova, 110 km from Turnu Severin (above) by the DN6 (the 17th century fortified monastery at Strehaia, 62 km from Craiova, is worth an en route stop), and about 240 from Bucharest via Pitesti (A1, then DN65).

The spot that visitors to Craiova make for is the Ban's House (Casa Baniei) in Strada Matei Basarab. The Turkish title "Ban" was given to local governors whether or not they were directly appointed by the Turks. The house itself was built in 1699 and today houses the well-displayed Dolj County Museum.

Craiova boasts a university, and its Art Gallery (in Calea Unirii) includes a number of Brancusi's works in its collection, housed in an elegant turn-of-the century mansion. The 15th century church in Gradina Trandafirilor (The Rose Garden) is one of the town's oldest buildings. But little else has survived Craiova's frequent disaster – the devastating earthquake of 1790, the plague of 1795, the burning of the entire town by Turks in 1802, the peasants' revolt of 1907, and disturbances resulting from strikes by Craiova's oil and railway workers in 1933–34. Today Craiova's the region's main transport centre, with direct rail routes to Bucharest on one side and Timisoara (Chapter Ten) on the other.

The important Danube port of Calafat lies 80 km southwest of Craiova. It's an unprepossessing spot, but it gives you an insight into the extraordinary importance that the Danube could have as a major transport artery. We've virtually renounced water transport in Britain, but plans have been made on the other side of Europe to link huge areas from the Volga and Vistula to the Rhine and the Danube with modern canals and improved river connections. The Dobrogea's Danube Canal (Chapter Five) and the vast Iron Gates storage lake (above) form vital parts of this system, and also link Eastern and Central Europe to ports all round the Black Sea. Like the Mississippi over much of its course the Danube's quite large enough for sea-going vessels.

A ferry carries traffic across the Danube from Calafat to Vidin in Bulgaria.

Turnu Magurele, 130 km east of Calafat by the DN54A (DN54 from Corabia) and 135 km southwest of Bucharest by the DN8, is the next main Danube port downstream. It has no passenger conection with the Bulgarian town of Nikopol on the river's opposite bank.

The next major crossing's at Giurgiu, 64 km by road due south from Bucharest (DN5). Here there's a double-decker bridge that's just about the ugliest structure I've ever seen. Giurgiu must also be one of Europe's most polluted spots. Even twenty years ago I remember it as constantly filled with yellow-brown, repulsive-smelling haze. A little over half-way to Bucharest, however, a turning from Calugareni takes you 15 km eastward to the important Comana Nature Reserve, with its Turkey oak forest, wild peonies, plentiful wild boar and deer, and the varied mashland flora and fish.

When you see the vast Danube at Giurgiu – the bridge is 2200 m long – you notice an odd thing. On the Bulgarian side it has a high bank. On the Romanian side the land's flat and has to be protected from flooding by levees constructed in the 19th century. This is true over much of the Danube's course – except that in some stretches it used to flood over both its banks, and not just once a year but twice.

Navigating on a river with innumerable shifting sandbanks and islands, and with indeterminate channels during parts of the year, was almost impossible till flood controls were built and buoyed – around 1830. The river till then was more a communications barrier than a major artery – and it was always an effective frontier.

Armies might – and frequently did –

follow its right (southern) bank in the days before effective roads existed (hence the strategic importance of right-bank hilltop settlements such as Belgrade in Yugoslavia and Mohacs and Buda in Hungary), but crossing the river was never easy till surprisingly recent times. The Giurgiu bridge was completed only in 1954. By a nice coincidence the place where the even more modern (and enormously more attractive) Danube road bridge has been built – Giurgeni (Chapter Five) – took its name from Giurgiu emigres many long years ago.

Silistra, some 140 km WSW of Bucharest by the DN3 (via Calarasi), is another harbour-town and jumping-off point for ferries across the huge Danube, taking you both to Bulgaria and into the southern Dobrogea. The DN3 continues to Mangalia. But its dull, flat route from Bucharest is hardly likely to be popular with tourists.

The same applies to most of the roads and virtually all the towns in the Danube Plain, as we found when we set out for Moldavia in Chapter Four.

Here is a map of the Bucharest Metro, specially drawn to help you.

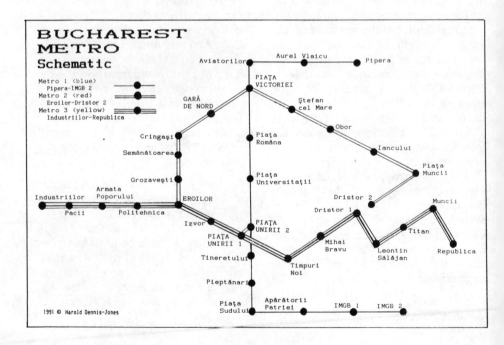

12. Background to Romania

There's a lot in Romania that's different from Western countries, and a lot that Western visitors don't expect. At the same time Romania's cultural links with the West are closer than most people imagine – particularly people whose knowledge comes from the Western media's postwar distortions. Understanding these contradictions involves considerable knowledge of the country and its history. We can give only an outline here.

Political History

Archaeological excavations show that Romania's territory has been inhabited for at least 100,000 years. When written history begins it was occupied by a nation which the Greeks called Getae and the Romans Daci (Dacians). They were a prosperous Thracian people with a centralised, well-organised government and high levels of skills. They traded extensively with Greek settlements established on the Black Sea coast from the 7th century BC on. They fought off invasions by the Persians in 514 BC, by Alexander of Macedon in 335 BC, and by his successor Lysimachus, whom they defeated and captured in 292 BC. They were conquered by the Roman Emperor Trajan in AD 106 only after a very carefully-planned and hard-fought campaign. The Romans had taken over the Greeks' Black Sea settlements and knew the Dacians' inland kingdom well.

Roman historians' written campaign accounts have mostly been lost. But we have fascinating pictorial details of the fighting in the bas-reliefs of Trajan's Column (casts were erected in Rome, Carthage, and Byzantium; there's a plaster copy in London's Victoria and Albert Museum) and the Tropaeum Trajani at Adamclisi in the Dobrogea (Chapter Five).

Although the later Roman Emperor Aurelian continued to stamp *Dacia Felix* (Prosperous Dacia) on his coins – a major public relations outlet for Roman Emperors – he had to withdraw his troops and administrators south of the Danube in AD 271. Archaeological remains suggest however that only a Roman minority left. The region remained romanised and large areas north of the Danube were intermittently under direct Roman control until the mid-6th century.

By that time Dacia was already being invaded by nomadic Germanic tribes and newcomers from Asia and the East European steppes. They included Vandals, Gepidae, Goths, Ostrogoths, Visigoths, Huns, Lombards, and finally Avars and other Slav tribes. The Slavs were the most numerous, but even they appear to have been successfully absorbed by the Roman-Dacian population, much as the Romanised Gauls of France assimilated the Germanic Franks to produce modern France. They added a lot of Slav words to the Dacians' Latin but did not change the language's basic structure.

By the 10th century, after further invasions by Magyars, Pechenegs, and Cumans, rudimentary small Romanian states were beginning to emerge. These eventually coalesced into the Principalities of Transylvania, Wallachia (or Muntenia), Moldavia, and Dobrogea (Dobrudja in its Slavic form), but slowly and only after centuries of confusion and conflict.

It's difficult for us to imagine this area's life in medieval-feudal days, when great landowners controlled everything on estates that might be scattered over half Europe, when the most powerful kings and barons exercised control over less powerful but always rebellious neighbours, continuous rivalry and fighting went on between them all, battles were often fought far from what we think of as the leaders' home bases, peaceful migrants settled wherever land or work was available, and stronger aggressors (eg, Tatars, Turks, Poles, Hungarians, Teutonic Knights) might appear at any moment. That was how things were in Romania when the Ottoman Turks first raided Wallachia in 1369 and how they continued for many later centuries.

All I can do to summarise this period is to mention a few outstanding characters and the actions which made them memorable. You'll find these names repeated constantly in Romania. People there have far clearer knowledge of their nation's history than we of ours.

First, however, I must mention that as early as 1141 the Hungarian King Geza II began encouraging German-speaking Saxon merchants (later granted special privileges denied to Romanians) to settle in Transylvanian towns. In the next century Hungarian-speaking Szeklers (Szekelyek in Hungarian, Secui in Romanian) were established as frontier guards in other parts of Transylvania. The descendants of both are still there.

The country's smaller ethnic minorities include descendants of Serbs who fled the Turks' advance in Serbia (14th century on), Turks, Tatars, Slovaks, a small number of Jews (the majority of those who survived WWII emigrated years ago to Israel), and a large number of gipsies.

Mircea the Old (Mircea cel Batrin) ruled Wallachia from 1386 to 1418. He consolidated and extended his own power and kept the Turks at bay while first Petru I (1375–1391) and later Roman I, Stefan I, and **Alexandru cel Bun** (Alexander the Good: 1400–1432) of Moldavia were fighting on the side of Wladislaw II Jagiello, King of Poland (1386–1432), against both Hungary and the Teutonic Knights. Mircea concluded an anti-Ottoman treaty with **Sigismund of Luxembourg**, King of Hungary (1387–1437), King (1410–1437) and later Emperor (1433–1437) of the Holy Roman Empire, and King of Bohemia (1420–1437).

Iancu de Hunedoara, as the Romanians call him (the Hungarians know him as **Hunyadi Janos**, and also claim him as a national hero), was an outstanding figure in an age of leaders larger than life. Ban of Severin (from 1438), Voivode (Count or Prince) of Transylvania (1441–1448), and Regent of Hungary for the under-age King Laszlo (1446–1456), he led an army of Hungarians, Czechs, Poles, Wallachs, and Germans against the Turks (the French, Aragonese, Venetians, and the Papacy had earlier declined to join him), and died of the plague at Zemun, just outside

Belgrade, which was being attacked by the Turks. They had conquered Constantinople (Byzantium) in 1453, putting an end to the Byzantine Empire.

In Janos Hunyadi's absence the defence of Southern Transylvania was entrusted to **Vlad Tepes** (Vlad the Impaler), Son of Vlad Dracul, Prince of Wallachia, but born in Sighisoara in Transylvania, Vlad became Voivode of Wallachia from 1456 to 1462 and again in 1476. He spent most of the intervening years imprisoned in Visegrad and elsewhere – we do not know why – by Janos Hunyadi's son, whom we call **Matthias Corvinus** (Matyas Korvin in Hungarian, Matei Corvin in Romanian), the greatest of all Hungary's kings (1458–1490).

Vlad Tepes scored brilliant victories against the Turks in Wallachia and beyond the Danube in 1461 and 1462. But because he was also obliged to deal with rebellious Hungarian-speaking Szeklers and German-speaking Saxons in Transylvania he became the media's first-ever victim when printing was still a novelty. The Germans sent back to Germany lurid stories of his executions by impaling (fairly normal in those days). These were embellished and published as sensational booklets – suitably illustrated with woodcuts, of course, Vlad himself used the name "Draculea" (probably intended to mean "Son of Dracul"). Bram Stoker found copies of these booklets in the British Museum Library (where they still are) and used the name "Dracula" in his own even more sensational (and knowingly inaccurate) novel.

Matthias Corvinus meanwhile had in 1443–44 penetrated Turkish-held country as far as Sofia, Bulgaria's modern capital, and Varna, its Black Sea port. In 1452, just before Constantinople's fall, he offered the Byzantine Emperor an alliance. It was refused. Matthias also had to suppress revolts in Transylvania by Szeklers in 1465 and by Szeklers, Hungarian aristocrats, and German merchants in 1467. Further, he found it necessary to wage war – unsuccessfully – against Moldavia, which was then allied to Poland but under attack from Turks and their Tatar allies.

Moldavia had come under the control of another of this period's great leaders, **Stephen the Great** (Stefan cel Mare, Voivode (Prince) of Moldavia 1457–1504). His greatest victory over the Turks, in 1475, was acclaimed throughout Europe. But requests for help from European sovereigns went unanswered. Combating Turks aided sometimes by Tatars and sometimes by Wallachians, he was at times supported by the Poles but ended by having to fight the Polish kings Casimir IV Jagiellor and John Albert – with Hungarian help.

The Turks' conquest of the Crimea in 1475 destroyed the Tatar's base there and made them a constant threat to Romania. To counter this Stephen ordered the construction of numerous monastery-fortresses controlling the valley routes leading into the Carpathians and providing refuges in time of need for surrounding villages (notably Voronet, Neamt, and Putna). Later leaders continued this policy.

The last of Romania's great medieval figures was **Mihai Viteazul** (Michael the Brave). He was Voivode of Wallachia from 1593 to 1601 and of Transylvania from 1599 to 1600. Elected Voivode of Moldavia for a time in 1600, he was the first to unite the main Romanian principalities.

Like Iancu de Hunedoara he fought

the Turks as far away as Sofia. But his position at home was never secure. He became Voivode of Transylvania and of Moldavia only by defeating the holders of those positions. The Hungarian nobility of Transylvania disliked his support of the Romanian peasants. The Poles wanted him removed from Moldavia. In 1601, after helping the Habsburg forces defeat the Polish-backed claimant to the Voivodate of Transylvania, he was murdered on the orders of the Italian-born Habsburg general, George Basta.

By now Romania's position was changed. The Turks had captured Buda, the Hungarian kings' capital, in 1541, and were clashing directly with the Austrian Habsburgs, whose capital, Vienna, they were to besiege in 1683. In 1552 they occupied the Banat, the flat area southwest of the Carpathian ring (capital Timisoara). They never formally occupied Wallachia and Moldavia. But from about 1600 on they exercised controlling influence there, partly through prominent Greeks and occasionally other nationals from Constantinople's Phanar district. From 1710 till they were forced in 1878 to abandon nearly all their European territories, the Turks were regarded by the European powers as Romania's real rulers.

Transylvania, though paying tribute to the Porte, as did Wallachia and Moldavia, somehow suffered far less interference. In fact, the 17th century saw it at the height of its prosperity and brilliance. But immediate political control veered between the Polish Bathory family and the Hungarian Bethlens, with the Austrian Habsburgs trying constantly to gain a footing there. Stefan Bathory, the great Polish king, when elected King in 1575, continued also as Voivode of

Transylvania. In 1608 Gabriel Bethlen (Bethlen Gabor to Hungarians) promoted himself from Governor to Prince of Transylvania.

By 1691, however, Transylvania's real rulers were the Habsburgs. They appoined the Governor – a situation formally recognised by the Porte in 1699. That year saw also the last serious Polish attack on Moldavia. It was made by King Jan Sobieski. From now until 1878 it is the Habsburgs, the Turks, and the Russians who decide Romania's fate. As the Porte weakened Vienna advanced. In 1718 they took over the Banat and Oltenia, Wallachia's western province (Chapter Eleven), and started settling Germans in the Banat. In 1775 the Turks gave them the Bucovina, Moldavia's most northerly part (Chapter Six).

Life in Romania continued uneasy and difficult. The Turkish Empire was breaking up. So was Romania's old order. In 1784 a peasant revolt more massive than any before broke out in Transylvania. Led by Horea, Closca, and Crisan, it was brutally suppressed. In 1821 Tudor Vladimirescu led a revolt against the Phanariot regime. He was defeated and executed. The Turks however replaced the Phanariots with native Romanians in 1824. One result of the 1828–29 Russo-Turkish War was increased freedom for Romania, though still considered Ottoman territory.

As in much of Europe, 1848 brought widespread rising against the relics of feudalism. In Romania it was confused by fighting between Austria and Hungary, by revolts against both Hungarian and Austrian governments, and by dissension between Hungarian and Romanian rebels, and was finally suppressed by the combined efforts of

Turks, Austrians, and Russians (now anxious to move into the vacuum created by the Turkish Empire's decline).

In 1864 Romanian peasants were (a little theoretically) released from serf-like obligations to landowners, the metric system was introduced, and new legal systems established. In the following year the Transylvanian Diet (Parliament, representing the wealthier classes) voted the region's annexation to Hungary. The Romanian deputies lodged a formal protest, but without effect. The Emperor Franz Josef prorogued the Diet *sine die*, effectively ending the region's quasi-independence.

A century previously the Austrian Empress Maria Theresa's officials had calculated that 66% of Transylvania's population was Romanian, 22% Hungarian and Szekler, and 12% Saxon German. Nevertheless, in 1867, when the Austro-Hungarian "Dual Kingdom" was established, "Greater Hungary", as people now call it, was allocated the whole of Transylvania, Slovakia (a large part of modern Czechoslovakia), what is now the Yugoslav Autonomous Province of Vojvodina, and most of the present Yugoslav Republic of Croatia. In 1879 the Hungarian Parliament passed a law making Hungarian the sole language to be used in its schools. Earlier efforts to subject the Orthodox Church to Catholic rule, going back to 1697, had been greatly resented. Bitterness still bedevils Romanian-Hungarian relations.

In 1877 Czarist Russia declared war on the Ottoman Empire and was joined by Romania, who proclaimed her independence and launched a vigorous and successful attack on the Turkish army at Plevna. The London *Times* and many other papers throughout Europe expressed unbounded admiration. The following year the Congress of Berlin, attended by all Europe's Great Powers, recognised the independence of many Turkish-occupied areas, including Romania. That meant just Moldavia (less the Bucovina) and Wallachia; Transylvania still belonged to Austria-Hungary. Leopold II of Belgium had been offered the throne of Romania in 1866, but had refused. Carl of Hohenzollern-Sigmaringen was proposed in his place and crowned King Carol I in 1881.

Liberation from Turkish rule did not bring peace and prosperity. Efforts were made to extend what little industry already existed. But there was unrest in the countryside, culminating in a large-scale rebellion based on a demand for land in 1907 (1864's promises had not been honoured). Romania became involved in the Second Balkan War of 1913 (between former Turkish territories, liberated in 1878) and then, despite attempts at neutrality and King Carol's efforts to have Romania side with Germany in WWI, declared war on Austria–Hungary in 1916 and was promptly attacked by Bulgars, Austrians, Germans, and Turks. The country was badly mauled till the Marasesti victory (Chapter Six).

The Trianon Peace Treaty of 1920 finally recognised Romania's right to the Banat, Bucovina, and Transylvania. It also established Yugoslavia and Czechoslovakia as separate, independent countries. But Romania wasn't out of the wood. 1922–28 were relatively peaceful years, with a considerable increase in industrialisation and improvements in living standards. Then came the Great Depression. Strikes and protests led to the establishment of the Nazi-backed Iron Guard, which gradually took control of the country, aligning it with the Axis powers. Eventually it forced King Carol II's abdication in 1940. His son Mihai succeeded him and Romania entered the war on Germany's and Italy's side. On 23 August 1944 however (a date commemorated in innumerable Romanian street-names) armed rebellion overthrew the government. The USSR granted a prompt armistice, which allowed Romania to turn its weapons against the occupying Axis powers. By 25 October the country was free of invaders.

But there was still no real peace, Stalin had decided that Romania should be a subject state. In 1946's first postwar election, which everyone now claims was rigged, the Communists and their allies were credited with a fraction under 80% of the votes. In 1948 Gheorghe Gheorghiu-Dej was elected General Secretary of the Romanian Communist Party's Central Committee, and a new Constitution adopted. From 1948 on the Party, under various names, acquired increasingly dictatorial powers, with the Central Committee taking decisions and a Parliament elected purely from Party candidates meeting only occasionally to approve them.

Gheorghiu-Dej died in 1965 and Nicolae Ceausescu was chosen to succeed him. In 1974 he had himself elected the country's first President. The extraordinary story of the twenty-five-year tyranny exercised by himself and his all-but-illiterate wife, Elena, would be well worth telling. But, believe it or not, as I write this the Romanian authorities are asserting that all documents are secret and no one has the right to see them.

Romanians have at last achieved liberty and the right to democratic government. But they hardly know even the words' meanings, and certainly have never had any experience of either's reality. Will they choose to be ruled by reformed Communists? Or allow in Westerners who see Romania's excessively low wages as a good opportunity for high profits? Or will their natural good sense, gentleness, and humanity find some middle way?

The world of the mind

Stupid arrogance makes many Westerners believe that because countries like Romania are technologically less advanced than us their citizens are all ignorant incompetents.

We would do well to remember, when we write the date, that the calculation, accepted worldwide, of Christ's death as having occurred in the 753rd year after the foundation of Rome was made by a Bishop of Tomi (modern Constanta), that oil-drilling equipment and railway locomotives are among Romania's most profitable exports, that at Montesson near Paris in 1906 the Romanian Traian Vuia managed to fly one of the world's first heavier-than-air machines (which he'd built himself), that N. Paulescu (1869–1931) introduced us to insulin, and that Anghel Saligny's magnificent Cernavoda railway bridge (still in use) was Europe's longest and the world's third longest (17 km, over 10 miles) when built in 1895.

Romania has never possessed the industrial support necessary for technological inventiveness and technological success, which we tend to imagine is what makes a nation "great". On the other hand it can claim a general standard of culture which many wealthier nations might envy, and a level of folk culture that is remarkable.

Most of the country was precluded till 1878 from joining Europe's academic and cultural activities by what was effectively Turkish occupation. Prosperous seventeenth-century Transylvania, on the other hand, produced more than its share of fine baroque buildings, scholarship, and excellent Western music (try, for instance, the Hungarian record company Hungaroton's LP SPLX 12047 *Renaissance Music in Transylvania*). Bucharest had its first symphonic concert, with works by Beethoven, Mozart, and Haydn, only in 1866.

By that time, as Turkish power declined, Romanian intellectuals were treating Paris as their Mecca. Nine hundred of them fought with the Communards in 1870. It was in Paris that Constantin Brancusi (1876–1957), "the father of modern sculpture", made his name (do, please, pronounce it correctly), and where the playwright Eugen Ionescu (b.1909) has spent most of his life. French is *every* educated older Romanian's second language. Innumerable French words have been taken into modern Romanian – if a *pieton* (pedestrian) bumps into you on the *trotoar* (pavement) of the *bulevard* he says *pardon*, imitating French pronunciation as best he can.

Though largely ignorant of West European music till the Ottoman Empire's last decades the Romanians quickly showed themselves as proficient in it as in their own very different tradition. Verdi wrote the title part of *Tosca* (1900) for the Romanian Hariclea Darclee. George Enescu (1895–1955) became world-famous as violinist (he was one of the young Menuhin's teachers) and also composer.

If Romania's outstanding singers and instrumentalists have been less noticeable in the West in recent years one reason has been that the Communist authorities took 90% of their gross earnings in tax. A tenor who could command $15,000 for three night's performances in New York in the 1970s found it unattractive to receive only $1500 for himself and to have to pay, maybe, his fare and hotel bills out of that. Some Romanian artistes however who have settled in the West, such as Ileana Cotrubas, enjoy worldwide fame and respect.

They themselves are usually the first to recognise that a large part of their skill stems from the enormous quantity and tremendously high standards of Romania's village musicians. When I gave a lecture on Romanian folk music at Harvard University John Milton, Professor of Music, interrupted me after my first taped illustration and asked for details of the singer. I said it would take some time to dig them out of my notes; she was just a village singer. "You mean she's not nationally famous?" asked John. "No", I replied. A girl student sitting in the front row gaped in wide-eyed astonishment. Shaking her head sadly, she said: "I'm majoring in singing. But I'll never sing like *that*".

The breadth of musical interest beggars belief. In 1978 a competition was held to choose a "Song for Romania" celebrating a century of liberation from Turkish rule. Any group could enter – from schools, factories, villages, army units, student clubs, anyone. Eighty-six *thousand* entries flooded in, and the winners were from an unknown village.

Understandably, Romania was in the

forefront of early steps in ethnomusicology, the study of traditional, non-Western music. Even before Bartok had begun his meticulous recording of village musicians in parts of the "Greater Hungary" of his day. Romanian folklorists had been at work. Constantin Brailoiu became the best-known of them. Some recent scholars, especially in the USA, seem bent on belittling Brailoiu's reputation. That's a pity, since the relative parts played by Bartok, Brailoiu, the composer Kodaly, and many other researchers can't be known till all the recordings they made in the first decades of this century and the huge quantity of accompanying notes have ben studied and analysed. Most of the material is held by Budapest's Institute of Ethnography, awaiting what to the West would be the tiny amounts of cash needed for the work.

Standards in the other folk arts are similar to music's. I've recorded Romanian village boys declaiming the poetry of their traditional New Year plays with all the resonance and power of a top British Shakespearean actor. The fact that this anonymous traditional verse is capable of being spoken in this way is itself telling. Many researchers have commented on the beauty of Romanian folksongs' anonymous texts and of the folk legends recorded from village story-tellers.

I have similarly gaped open-mouthed at the woodcarving skills of unknown Maramures countryfolk, at superb handwoven fabrics produced on unbelievably primitive looms by ordinary village women, and at icons painted on glass by village artists.

The recent rush to the towns, the wish to keep up with the Western Joneses and their transistorised music, the disastrous standards of bureaucratically controlled industrial design and even shoddier production have befouled this natural taste and love of beauty. But almost every Romanian seems still to dream of one day becoming some form of artist – if not in music then in words or visual arts.

That may sound exaggerated. If you visit the Museum of Village Technology at Dumbrava Sibiului or the Rasinari museum and Craft School you'll realise that it isn't. As often as not the simplest, most everyday handmade objects in the Dumbrava museum are extraordinarily beautiful. That is how man works when not driven by his own or someone else's greed.

The Rasinari Craft School's products are often overwhelming but – inevitably – expensive. Some cheaper stuff in tourist souvenir shops is attractive. Some isn't.

Industry, technology, and politics

If you visit only Romania's inland towns you risk thinking the whole country is run-down and badly in need of renovation. In the countryside however you realise that Romania's basically a peasant country with a strong peasant culture that has had lumps of more or less modern industry, including pretty inefficient industrialised farming in the plains, ineffectually welded onto it. It isn't that the Romanians lack ability or willingness. Far from it. They're capable of turning out excellent products. But everything – almost – has been unbelievably badly managed over the last forty years.

How quickly changes can be brought

about no one can say. Political and economic uncertainties are rife. And no one can see which way to go.

But whatever problems lie ahead we should not forget past achievements. Constantin Brincoveanu, Prince of Wallachia (1688–1714), must surely count as one of Europe's great architect-builders, and Dimitrie Cantemir, Prince of Moldavia (1673–1723), as one of our great humanists. The difficulty the Romanians face is that Westerners, even academics, seem reluctant even to look at what has been achieved east of Vienna.

Romania and Europe

To treat the Romanians as being somehow not quite part of Europe – which is the attitude many Western commentators still take – is a gratuitous insult. Romanian scholarship, when not distorted by an uneducated dictator's dogma, can and does hold its own with Western Europe's best. There's much in Romanian education which we could learn from. Historically they have contributed enormously to Europe's united survival, as this chapter's historical summary shows. A different aspect of Romanian culture however reveals a marked difference from Western Europe.

Despite the country's large Hungarian minority, divided mainly between the Roman Catholic and Reformed Churches, and other smaller minorities such as the Protestant Germans, the bulk of Romania belongs to the eastern Orthodox Church – or at least grew up with an Orthodox background. Though Christian churches existed during the Roman occupation of Dacia the country later shared the Christianisation of the eastern Slav lands by St Cyril and St Methodius and their disciples. This doesn't seem important until you start discussing something like Romania's current political and social problems with Romanian friends.

A basic Protestant idea is that each of us has an individual obligation to make up our own minds about what is right and what is wrong, and a personal obligation to take whatever action may be necessary to suppport what we consider right. This is almost totally alien to the Orthodox mind. Communality is the keystone of Orthodox belief. No hint of any individual-stressing Reformation has ever shaken the Orthodox churches. Many still believe that even being so individual as to sing in separate harmonised parts (as the reforming Luther encouraged lay Western churchgoers to do) is wrong.

Even doing your own thing to the extent of singing different harmonic lines wasn't tolerated till recently. The Romanian Orthodox Church began permitting harmony only about 1900. The Armenian Apostolic (Orthodox) Church allowed it only in the 1960s.

West European technology, and indeed Western civilisation as a whole, depends to a very large extent on innovators who refuse to accept what everyone else does and believes. Faced suddenly with a national political-social situation which demands that everyone think hard and make his/her own decisions, and act on the judgments made, the Romanians are finding life very difficult. So are some other East European countries. None of our commentators seems yet (June 1990) to have noticed that the only countries with sizable pockets of surviving Communist supporters are those with

Orthodox backgrounds – Romania, Bulgaria, the USSR and, to a lesser extent, Czechoslovakia (or rather Slovakia). In Romania, incidentally, Orthodox influence has been so strong, and the Church's part in the long battle for national identity and freedom so strong that banning it has been unthinkable.

The future threatens to be even tougher. Transylvania poses a more immediate and more explosive problem. Until you've spent time among ordinary Hungarians and ordinary Romanians you'll never grasp how bitter each side feels about the other.

The quarrel began centuries ago, as our historical summary shows. Modern Hungarians, even the gentlest and best educated, feel that they have the right to own and rule it because for centuries it belonged to Hungary – until the Western Powers (to quote the regular Hungarian version) tore it away from them after 1918. The Romanians maintain that they're entitled to Transylvania because their blood has always predominated there. Despite the figures from Maria Theresa's reign and her description of Transylvania as Austria's "Romanian province" the Hungarians retort that talk about Romanians' numerical predominance is a pack of lies: the Romanians have been deliberately settling Romanians there only since 1918 so as to claim the region.

You can't reason with either side so don't try. Keep clear of the argument. Non-committal noises are probably best.

The Romanians and you

Apart from possible arguments over Transylvania and the tensions which inevitably surface in overcrowded towns you'll find Romanians, especially in the countryside, almost too hospitable. If you go walking in the mountains almost everything with wheels will insist on your clambering aboard – even if it's a tractor whose cab is already bursting with outsize Romanian forestry workers or an overloaded cart pulled by a reluctant horse.

If you're invited into a country home for coffee or a drink – beware. The Romanian instinct is to pull out not a bottle but a case of wine for the "drink". "Coffee" is apt to mean a cup of coffee, several plates of pastries, and a bottle of wine or umpteen glasses of *tuica* (sweet plum brandy). Once, when I was invited to "take refreshments", I found myself doing battle with the largest seven-course meal I'd ever faced in my life. Declining what's put in front of you isn't polite.

Courtesy demands offering something in return. Western chocolate or chocolates are usually acceptable (keep them wrapped in a plastic mack or something similar). Ordinary Western soap (it doesn't have to be fancy) also goes over well. If you stay with a family the women will appreciate a packet of Wundaweb or an equivalent product. The realisation that miles of hem-stitching can be so easily avoided is greatly valued. You'll have to demonstrate how to use it though. If all else fails, take a photograph of your hosts – and remember to send them a print.

13. Practical Information

Before you leave If you've bought a package tour you should get as much information as you can about the places you'd like to visit – from travel agent, tour operator, and the Romanian National Tourist Office (address below). Tackle the NTO if you're travelling independently. If you're using a car a decent map is essential. Freytag & Berndt's *Romania/Bulgaria* is available in UK, and Carpathia's *Romania* in Hungary. The NTO's free map is not very detailed and isn't always easily available. If necessary, while in Bucharest barge into the Automobil Clubul Roman's (ACR's) HQ office and ask for maps of both Romania and Bucharest.

If you're travelling by public transport you'll probably have to make do with the information provided here for your advance planning, and rely for departure times, prices, etc on information obtained on the spot. But tackle the NTO well before you leave.

Visas are included in package tour prices, and can be obtained on arrival by independent travellers. You'll need to pay in sterling or other hard currency however. This means a minimum of £30 in cash. In practice, rather more than that – say £50 or £60 may be advisable, preferably mainly in £5 notes and with seven or eight £1 coins. You may need sterling for odd "dollar shop" purchases. Traveller's cheques can be used, of course. But banks aren't keen nowadays on small denominations, and you won't always get change in sterling in Romania.

You can't obtain Romanian currency (*lei*, singular *leu*, "lions") in Britain and you're not permitted to take any out of the country. In theory you can exchange surplus lei at the airport or frontier on departure. In practice this doesn't always work. Arrange to spend all your lei before reaching the frontier. Sterling oddments can be used if necessary at the airport.

Personal, baggage, and cash insurance is highly advisable. Package tourists should also cover themselves and their families against airport delays and the like. For car tourists a green card is essential and accident and breakdown insurance well worthwhile. There's no space to go into the intricacies of insurance policies here. The possible variations are a specialist subject. I can only say that after years of experimentation I settled a long time ago on Europ Assistance for my personal cover. Under their scheme you don't need to make any immediate payment yourself and recover the sums later from your insurers. One phone call or telex message to London brings all the help you need and Europ Assistance's agents pay bills on the spot (address below).

Take all the medicaments, cosmetics, suntan lotions, films, babyfood, and everything else of this sort that you might conceivably need. Don't rely on finding any of it in Romania (though it may sometimes be available in resorts' "dollar shops", where you pay in sterling or other hard currencies). If you're travelling independently (including by car) take also your own loo paper and soap – just in case.

Travelling to Romania by air is straightforward. Tarom Romanian Airlines operate direct from Heathrow to Bucharest. By rail you can take the Orient Express (the real Orient Express, which began operating well over a century ago) from Paris right through to Bucharest. It's more convenient from Britain however to travel via the Ostend-Vienna Express and change at Vienna onto the connecting Wiener Walzer Express for Budapest, where you can profitably break your journey. Second class compartments on the Orient Express sometimes come from rolling stock that has seen better days. Standards on the Ostend-Vienna Express and the Wiener Walzer are usually fine.

Budapest's beauty and cheapness is one good reason for stopping off there. Another is that if you book the final part of your rail trip in Hungary you benefit from huge governmental subsidies on rail travel between East European countries. A second-class return from Budapest to Bucharest booked in Budapest costs barely £10, including outward seat reservation. If you buy your ticket in Britain you pay well over £100 for this section.

Ticket clerks at Budapest's Keleti (West) Station, where most international trains arrive, rarely speak English, though many can cope in German. In case of need, go to the railway (not the tourist) information desk and ask them to write down on a piece of paper everything the international ticket clerk needs.

Senior Citizens' Rail Europe cards, obtainable for a small extra charge by anyone holding a British Senior Citizen Railcard, entitle you to 30% reductions as far as Hungary's further border, but not in Romania. InterRail Under-26 covers a month's travel throughout Europe and InterRail +26 (not Poland, Morocco, or Spain) a month or 15 days. These are notably cheap.

If you want to travel as cheaply as possible to Romania, go by Attila Tours coach from London to Budapest (address below). Like the train, this takes roughly 28 hours. And, like the train, the coach has an on-board loo and stops pretty frequently. Spend a night or two in Budapest; private-house accommodation need cost no more than £5 a night for b & b, with restaurant meals costing even less. Book your rail return to Bucharest (or whatever your Romanian destination is) soon after your arrival, especially if you want a couchette: there's a travel agency where language is no problem on Keleti Station, but couchette-booking may involve telexes and time. All you'll need for your return is to make seat and/or couchette reservations in Romania.

In 1991 discounted air returns to Bucharest cost about £160 (Budapest £180!). APEX rates started at £276, with full-rate tickets above £400. Ordinary London-Bucharest rail return sets you back £338. London-Budapest rail return costs £251, with Senior Citizens Rail Europe cardholders charged £182. InterRail +26 (for over 26s) costs £235 for a month, £175 for 15 days. London-Budapest coach returns cost £85-£135 according to season (return to Bucharest thus barely £100!).

Coach and air travel (unless you pay the very high full air ticket prices) involves fixing travel dates well in advance, and keeping to them. One advantage of rail travel is that your return ticket is valid on any day for three months.

Inside Romania independent travellers' only source of general information is the Tourist Offices maintained by the Ministry of Tourism in the resorts, all county towns, and other main towns. Unfortunately, these are more geared to selling coach tours and the like than to providing the innumerable details independent travellers want. Not all have English speakers. But try them.

For travel information you'll either have to get someone to phone for you or go to the bus station or the railway station yourself (in Bucharest to the railway "agency" close to the Nord main terminus or to the older base in Strada Brezoianu, off the Bulevard Gheorghe Gheorghiu-Dej; internaional tickets, seat reservations, etc are available only at the latter).

If you want a seat on a country bus book your ticket in advance at the bus's starting-point; seat reservation is included. If you board at an intermediate stop expect to stand. The same applies to trains. Booking a bus ticket or a rail ticket may involve choosing the right counter for your destination.

In towns there's a flat rate for buses and trams – in Bucharest 3 lei a journey. Before setting off, you buy tickets from newsstands near stops or – sometimes – from the driver. On the Bucharest Metro you put 2 lei in an automatic gate under the eagle eye of a Metro employee. This allows you to travel anywhere on the system until you pass a notice saying IESIRE (exit) or TRECEREA OPRITA (no entry), watched by another eagle-eyed male or female official. Journeys from Piata Unirii, at the very centre of the Metro network cost only 1 leu.

Virtually all public transport is crowded – apart from early morning bus/tram or Metro travel and rail journeys from provincial towns starting very early.

As even first class railway travel is inexpensive – about £4 for 150 miles – you can ensure a little space for yourself, at least inside your compartment, by booking first class. That doesn't mean the corridor won't be crammed, nor that the lavatories will be clean and provided with toilet paper – at least until promised improvements take effect. A decade or two ago Romanian Railways (Caile Ferate Romame, or CFR) enjoyed a high reputation among railway buffs. It's uncertain how soon old levels can be regained.

Air is an inexpensive alternative to long-distance domestic rail journeys. You can fly from Bucharest (Baneasa, not Otopeni airport) to Suceava, Tulcea, Constanta, Brasov, Sibiu, Cluj-Napoca, Timisoara, Arad, Oradea, Satu Mare, and Baia Mare. The Bucharest-Constanta return fare costs about £35 return.

Self-drive car hire can be arranged through tourist offices in major towns, through your hotel, or in advance through international car hire firms. Fly-drive package tours also exist.

Taxis aren't always easy to find. Your hotel should be able to order one for you, but they aren't always available even at the larger provincial railway stations. In Bucharest take only official taxis with official registration numbers and taximeters. You're liable to have problems with "pirates".

Accommodation on package tours compares well with what you'll get in other countries. That applies to meals as well as rooms. The only criticism is that there's usually a lack of genuine Romanian food available. The Romanian authorities say this is because a lot of Romanian cooking involves considerable food-handling – which adds greatly to food-poisoning danger. Every resort however has at least one restaurant specialising in local dishes.

In 1991 the hotel list available from the National Tourist Office included only hotels run by the Ministry of Tourism. It omitted scores of smaller establishments operated by local cooperatives and the like, as well as the Hanul lui Manuc, Bucharest's reconstructed 19th century caravanserai, which could be very pleasant were its large courtyard not used mainly as a sort of open-air bar.

Independent travellers wanting to book hotel accommodation can get help from tourist offices in the larger towns, who may also be able to make private house accommodation bookings in some cases. But the system wasn't properly operative in 1990 – hardly surprising, since private house accommodation had been illegal for some twenty years. In case of need a taxi driver or almost anyone you meet will find you a bed somewhere if you indicate, by signs if necessary, that you need somewhere to sleep. Putting your hands together and leaning your head on them is pretty universally understood. Fix the price in advance. You can do this by having it written down. The inescapable bits of Romanian language you'll need are given below.

If you're travelling by car and camping, use either organised campsites or land where the owners indicate you can camp *and where there'll be someone constantly available to keep an eye on your gear while you're away.* The Romanians won't steal anything. Gipsies may.

Travelling with a trailer or motor caravan can be an ideal way of seeing Romania. You can stop almost anywhere, and you'll find the local people embarrassingly hospitable and helpful. I once woke up in a motor caravan on a piece of land beside a little used road to find a whole family patiently waiting with our breakfast.

Campsite lists are available from the NTO. If you plan to use mountain huts, ask locally about availability, especially in high summer. Arriving unannounced is normal however.

Shopping for food and drink may present problems if you're camping or travelling independently and relying partly on picnics. Bread, vegetables and, usually, milk, eggs, and sometimes cheese are normally available in town shops and markets (many villages have no shops). Fish, and sometimes meat, aren't. If you want fresh meat buy it whenever you see it being sold (on my last trip this often involved a bit of queueing). Delicatessen meats and sausages are far more readily available and will, of course, keep well. The supply of soft drinks other than spa water such as *Borsec* (from the Moldavian spring) is limited – and even spa water can suddenly stop being available. Biscuits can be bought for snacks. They usually contain little sugar or sweeteners – which is probably healthy, but not much to Western tastes. Various savoury pasties, hot dogs, etc, as well as ice cream, are sold in the streets of Bucharest and other towns.

Every sort of liquor other than some beers (local brews only) can inexplicably vanish from the shops. Normally however you've a pretty plentiful supply of excellent table reds and whites, and a few sparkling wines. The local firewater, *tuica*, is a sweetish plum brandy, served hot in cold weather as you enter the house, when it's specially welcome. Romanians also produce their own vermouth (*vermut*). If you like sweet aperitifs you'll find a drink called *Amalfi* (half tuica and half local sweet vermouth) extremely relaxing after a long day on the road or walking or skiing in the mountains.

Markets start operating very early. Shops, if they're going to open (sometimes they don't), are working by 0900 or 0930 and usually close towards 18.00. Tourist offices are usually open by 09.00. Bus stations start work at 06.00 or earlier. Some main railway stations have trains going through and stay open all night. Bucharest's railway "agencies" are open from 07.00 till 20.00, and its Metro operates from 05.00 till midnight (see lists at all stations).

Romanian cuisine isn't much served in hotels, though resorts have speciality restaurants. Ordinary town restaurants naturally offer typical simple dishes, but hardly on the vast scale of a truly Romanian formal meal. Here starters could include various sorts of pork, egg, and offal dishes. In summer salads of uncooked vegetables, with only a little salt or olive oil added, might be placed beside them. The soup would be chosen from a range made from all sorts of vegetables, often containing pieces of meat. In the Danube Delta region

caviar or white caviar (from the male sturgeon) might be served for starters and the ordinary soup replaced by a fish soup reminiscent of bouillabaisse.

In a full meal that would perhaps be followed by *sarmale* – cabbage leaves stuffed with mince, accompanied by *mamaliga*, boiled maize virtually the same as Italian polenta. Alternatives would include *mititei* ("tiddlers", which they emphatically aren't: they're outsize bangers made of pure meat and grilled in their own fat), or *tocana* a meat stew with a lot of onion.

You might still have to face a large plate of roast meat – beef, pork, or lamb, or even a combination of them – possibly garnished with more vegetables. For desserts you'd have oriental sweetmeats such as *baclava*, or Viennese pastries, cheese pancakes, plum dumplings, etc. And you might be offered a fairly plain cheese as well.

Many dishes like this can be bought in town restaurants that Romanians themselves patronise. Prices are modest. £12 a day (say, $20) pays for all normal meals, including coffee and a glass of wine.

Telephone calls can be made from hotels, usually with a supplementary charge. Kiosks, where they exist, take 1 leu for local calls, 3 lei non-local. Dial only the code plus subscriber's number. International calls can be made only through the operator. You'll often find that going to the main post office's telephone section is your best bet for international or long-distance calls. Write the number down on a piece of paper and show it to the attendant. He/she will keep dialling the number until contact is made, and then connect the call to a cabin which will be indicated to you. The Romanian telephone network isn't particularly efficient, and numbers in some mountain areas still don't have automatic dialling.

Electricity is 220 volts, but you'll need a special plug or one of the "universal" adaptors.

Changing money Hotels and domestic air prices quoted here are what you pay at the "official" rate – booking through UK agents, for instance. Travelling independently you can save considerably by changing "hard" currency (traveller's cheques or cash) in legal "free"-rate exchange offices. They may give you two-and-a-half or even three times as many lei per pound or dollar, making lei prices considerably cheaper. Banks and other concerns operate these "free" exchange offices.

Romanians can buy hard currency at the "free" rate, so there's no point in patronising black marketeers. You can give Western currency (not cheques) to Romanian friends wishing to open hard currency accounts (minimum $100).

Prices are low but rising, so check all figures quoted here. Westerners' accommodation rates run from £20 to £40 ($32-$63) per person per night for double rooms with private baths in Bucharest (add 50% for single occupancy: de luxe up to £100 or $180). Equivalent prices in coastal resorts are roughly £10-£30, and in other towns £17-£25. Campsite chalets cost about £7. Aid workers and Romanians have special prices.

Public holidays are in the melting-pot following the revolution. National Day, 1 December, is the only one you can be certain of. In 1990 1 January (St Basil's Day – New Year's Day), Orthodox Good Friday and Easter Monday (different from ours), 1 May

(Labour Day) and, in some country districts, 15 August (Assumption Day) were treated as holidays.

Medical help can be obtained in every resort from a medical and first aid centre (usually labelled POLICLINIC) where minor accidents and ailments are treated free, and where prompt help is provided for more serious problems. Package tourists can also of course rely on their tour operators' reps for help and advice. Independent tourists have to rely on local doctors and hospitals, whose prices (if you're not insured) are very low, but whose equipment and medical stocks are woefully substandard. Europ Assistance-type medical insurance could prove useful. Its basic belief is that everyone is better treated by the medical system he/she's accustomed to, and that serious cases should be brought home if possible. Policies cover costs. *Take syringes to preclude AIDS.* On long stays beware minor infections.

Women on their own can normally rely on travelling unhassled except in Westerner-frequented resorts – provided they don't make a point of drawing attention to themselves.

Emergencies and disasters Your tour operator's rep will normally do everything that's needed. If you're on your own virtually everyone will do their best to help. The British Embassy in Bucharest will provide advice, addresses, etc, but the only practical help they're allowed to give is to advance you your fare home if you're broke.

Photography of bridges, railway workshops' interiors, frontiers and military installations is forbidden. Several airports have military sections, so be careful when you're in them. And be courteous to human subjects.

Addresses

Romanian National Tourist Office,
17 Nottingham St, London, W1M
3RD:
tel. 071 224-3692

Romanian National Tourist Office,
573 Third Avenue, New York,
NY 10016: tel. (212) 697-6971

Automobil Club Roman
Beloianis 27, Bucharest

Europ Assistance
Europ Assistance House, 252 High St,
Croydon, CR0 1NF: tel. 081 680-1234

Attila Tours
Persepolis House, 36A Kilburn High
Rd, London, NW6 5BU:
tel. 071 372-0470

Discounted air fares Try especially
Friendly Tours Ltd, Research
House, Fraser Rd, Perivale, Mdsx
UB6 7AQ: tel. 081 566-9040

Tour operators include **Balkan
Holidays, Duggan, Page & Moy,
Romanian Holidays, Saga,
Sunquest** and, in Dublin, **Balkan
Tours**. Other firms offer specialist
trips. **Friendly Tours** provide skilled
individual itineraries.

"Signed, Dracula" – one of the variations Vlad Tepes' secretaries used. This letter in
Latin, addressed to the nobles of Wallachia, begins (in the normal Latin way): "Nos,
Ladislaus Dragkulija, waiwada partium transalpinarum . . ." – We, Vlad Draculea,
voivode of the regions beyond the mountains [ie, Wallachia, mostly in the Danube Plain,
beyond the South Carpathian summits] . . .

Essential Romanian

Romanian's basic sounds The language is "phonetic". If you hear a word spoken clearly, you can write it accurately. The reverse isn't always possible because word-stress varies. When words end in consonants the stress falls mostly, but not invariably, on the last syllable. Otherwise on the last but one.

Alphabet k, q, w, and y are used only in foreign words (*kilometer, New York*). Consonants are pronounced as in English, except that j sounds like the s in leisure; ş sounds as -sh-; and ţ as -ts-. Before e or i c sounds -tch- and g -dge-. Otherwise, including before î or â, c is like -k-, and g like -gg-. gh and ch before -i or -e- are also "hard".

u sounds like -oo-. ă is pronounced roughly like English -er-, î as French -oeu- (â has the same sound as î, which replaced it in 1953 except in the words *România, român, românesc* = Romanian, and in old family names). A stressed e at the start of a word is pronounced ye-. The -i at the end of words is virtually unheard (like the e in the French word *signe*).

Two or more vowels coming together are all pronounced separately. They do not combine to form new sounds. One however predominates: the others are "soft". *Oradea* is hardly distinguishable from *Orada: seara* is hardly distinguishable from Italian *sera*.

Romanian's word-forms and basic grammar are still very close to their ancestral Latin, which makes notices etc easy to read if you know Latin, French, or Italian. Over the centuries however it has absorbed Slav and Turkish words.

It has also developed very differently from Western Romance (ie, Roman) languages. It still has masculine (m.), feminine (f.), and neuter (n.) nouns. All nouns have separate singular and plural forms: when the definite article (= the) is tacked onto nouns (it doesn't precede them) they all have two singular and two plural forms, and some have a third singular form. See **Nouns.**

The definite article can also be added to some adjectives describing nouns. In addition there is a sort of emphatic definite article, *cel, cea; cei, cele. Mihai Viteazul* = Michael the Brave, *Ştefan cel Mare* = Stephen the Great.

Possession is indicated by the "possessive article" *al, a; ai, ale* placed before the genitive-dative of general nouns – *Lacul al miresei* = The bride's lake – or by *lui* before a m. name – *Hanul lui Manuc* = Manuc's Inn.

Verb-tenses' endings vary, so that you put "I", "you", etc before verbs only for emphasis. With close friends you use the 2nd person singular ("thou") verb form, to others the 2nd person plural ("you"). To be even more formal you use *dumneavoastră* (= Your Excellency) with a 3rd person singular ("he") verb-form.

But all this is for interest rather than novice use. Bare vocabulary makes perfect sense. "Two tickets – second class – tomorrow – Suceava – train 392 – 13.28" is perfectly clear and totally understandable.

We have room here only for essential words.

Courtesies

Sir!	*domnul!*	Good evening! (from about 18.30)	*bună seara*
Madam!	*doamnă!*	Good night!	*noapte bună!*
Miss!	*domişoară!*	Goodbye!	*la revedere!*
Excuse me! (request)	*povtim!*	(I) thank you	*mulţumesc*
		(We) thank you	*mulţumim*
Excuse me! (apology)	*scusaţi! pardon!*	Yes	*da*
Good morning! (till c.09.30)	*bună dimineaţa!*	No	*nu*
		With pleasure	*cu placere*
Good day!	*bună ziua*	I don't understand	*nu înteleg*

Do you speak English?	*vorbiţi englezeşte?*
I don't speak Romanian	*'nu vorbim româneşte*

Numbers, days, dates, time

Number	*număr*
One, two, three, four,	*un (u), una, o; doi, două;*
five, six, seven, eight,	*trei; patru, cinci, şase,*
nine	*şapte, opt nouă*

Ten, eleven, twelve,	*zece, unsprezece,*
thirteen etc	*doisprezece, etc*
Twenty,	*douăzece,*
thirty,	*treizece,*
forty, etc	*patruzece, etc*

Twenty-one, twenty-two,	*douăzece şi un(a),*
etc	*douăzece şi doi*
One hundred, two	*o suta, două*
hundred, etc	*suta, etc*
One thousand, two	*o mie, două mii,*
thousand, etc	*trei mii*
One hundred thousand	*o suta de mii*
One million	*un milion*

First, second, third,	*primul, prima; al doilea,*
fourth, etc	*a doua; al treilea, a treia;*
	etc

Monday, Tuesday,	*luni, marţi*
Wed., Thurs.,	*miercuri, joi,*
Friday,	*vineri,*
Saturday	*sîmbătă,*
Sunday	*duminică*

January, February,	*ianuarie, februarie,*
March, April, etc	*martie, aprilie, mai, iunie,*
	iulie, august,
	septembrie, octobrie,
	novembrie, decembrie

Christmas, Easter,	*Craciun, Paşti,*
Assumption (15 Aug),	*Maria Hram,*
New Year	*Nou An*

Clock, watch	*ceas*
What time is it?	*ce ora eşte?*
	cît eşte ceasul?
Three o'clock	*ora trei*
Four fifteen, a quarter	*patru şi cinciprezece;*
past four	*patru şi un sfert*
Half past five,	*cinci şi jumătate;*
five thirty	*c. şi treizece*
A quarter to six,	*şase fără un sfert, cinci*
five forty-five	*şi patruzece şi cinci*

Minute	*minut*
Hour	*oră*
Day, days	*zi, zile*

Week	*săptămînă*
Month	*lună*
Morning	*dimineaţă*
Afternoon	*după-amiază*
Evening	*seară*
Night	*noapte*
Early (in day)	*devreme*
Late (in the day)	*tîrziu*

Yesterday	*ieri*
Day before y'day	*alaltăieri*
Today	*astazi, azi*
Tomorrow	*mîine*
Day after t.	*poimîine*
This evening	*astă seară*

Directions

Where is . . . ?	*unde eşte?*
(To the) left	*la stînga*
(To the) right	*la dreapta*
Straight on	*drept, direct*
First, second, third, etc	(see above)
Next	*următor*
Last	*ultim*
How far?	*ce distanţa eşte?*
(Very) near	*(foarte) aproape*
(Very) far	*(prea) departe*
Beginning	*început*
End	*capăt*
Crossroads	*răscruce*
Road junction	*intersecţie*
Main road	*rută*
Street	*stradă*
Footpath	*cale, potecă*
Road sign	*semn, indicator*
Bend (in road)	*curbă, cotitură*
In front (of)	*înainte (de)*
Behind	*înapoi (de)*

Notices

Open	*deschis*
Closed	*închis*
Entrance	*intrare, trecere*
Exit, way out	*ieşire*
Emergency exit	*i. de urgentă*
No admittance	*trecerea oprită*
One-way street	*sens unic*
Danger	*pericol*
(Road) works	*lucrări stradale*
Car park	*parcare*
No parking	*parcare interzisă*

Loos

Lavatory	*toaletă*
Ladies	*femeii, doamne*
Gents	*oameni, bărbaţi*
Free	*liber(ă)*
Occupied	*luat, ocupat*

Accommodation

Hotel	*hotel*
Campsite	*camping*
Chalet	*bungalow, cabană*
Bedroom	*cameră, dormitor*
Bathroom	*cameră de baie*
Bath	*baie*
Shower	*duş*
Hot, cold water	*apa, caldă a. rece*
Lift	*lift*
Staircase	*scară*

Food and drink

Restaurant	*restaurant*
Café	*bufete, cofetaria*
Snackbar	*bufete-expres*
Menu (list)	*menu*
Bill (=account)	*notă (de plată)*
Receipt	*chitanţă reţetă*
Breakfast	*micul dejun*
Lunch (midday)	*dejun*
Dinner (evening)	*cină*

Coffee, tea	*cafea, ceai*
Beer, wine	*bere, vin*
Red, white	*roşu, alb*
(Mineral) water	*apă minerala*
Fruit juice	*suc de fructe*
Cheers!	*noroc*

Starters	*minuturi, hors d'œuvres*
Fish	*peşte*
Meat	*carne*
Beef	*vacă*
Mutton	*oi*
Pork	*porc*
Chicken	*pui*
Egg, eggs	*ou, ouă*
Omelette	*omletă*
Vegetables	*legume*
Salad	*salata*
Bread	*piine*
Fruit	*fructe*
Cheese	*brinză*
Ice cream	*îngheţată*

General

How much does it cost?	*cît costă?*
This	*acesta*
That	*acela*
Is it possible?	*se poate?*
A lot	*mult*
A little	*mic, puţin*
More, less	*mai, mai puţin*
Enough	*destul*

Good, bad	*bun, rău*
Better, worse	*mai bun, mai rău*
Cheap	*ieftin*

(Too) expensive	*prea scump*
When?	*cînd?*
(at what time?)	*la ce oră?*
Where?	*unde?*
How?	*cum?*
I would like	*vreau*
We would like	*vrem*
To have (= own)	*a avea*
To be	*a fi*
To buy	*a cumpăra*
To (ex)change	*a schimba*
To go, to travel	*a merge, a călători*

And, or, but	*şi, sau, dar*
In, to, at	*în, la, la*
With, without	*cu, fără*
As far as, from	*pîna la, de la*
Thus, if, of	*aşa, dacă, de*
For, towards	*pentru, spre*
Now, then	*acum, atunci*
Here, there	*aici, acolo*
Name, word	*nume, cuvînt*
Newspaper	*ziar*
Magazine	*rivistă*

Travelling

Passenger(s)	*călător(i)*
The train for	*trenul pentru*
Bus	*autobuz*
Plane	*avion*
Boat, ferry	*barcă, bac*
Airport	*aeroport*
Station	*gară*
Harbour	*port*
Car	*auto(mobil)*
Cycle	*bicicletă*
Motor cycle	*motocicletă*

Departure	*sosire*
Arrival	*plecare*
Platform	*linie, peron*
Quay	*chei*
(Embarkation) gate	*poartă*

Ticket	*tichet, bilet*
Return ticket	*dus întors*
(Seat) reservation	*rezervaţie*
Seat(s), place(s)	*loc(uri)*
(Railway) car	*vagon*
Sleeping car	*vagon de dormit*
Couchette	*cuşetă*
First, second class	*clasă înfîia, c. al doua*
No smoking	*fumatul interzis*

Via	*prin*
Daily	*zilnic*
Does not run	*nu circulă*
Sundays	*dumenicile*
Public holidays	*sărbătorile legale*

Seasonal	*sezonier*
Station	*staţie*
Request stop	*facultativ*

Sightseeing
Church	*biserică*
Cathedral	*catedrală*
Museum	*muzeu*
Castle (fort)	*cetate*
Palace, mansion	*palat, casă*
Office	*birou*
Tower	*turn*
(Fortress) wall	*zid (fortificat)*

Shopping and money
Money	*bani (plur.)*
To change	*(a) schimba*
Exchange office	*birou de schimba*
Shop	*magazin*
Market	*tîrg*
To buy	*a cumpăra*
To sell	*a vinde*
Seller	*vînzator(a)*

Spare time
Cinema	*cinema*
Theatre	*teatru*
Concert hall	*sală de concert*
Beach	*plajă*
Excursion	*excursie*
Nightspot	*bar de noapte*
Holiday	*sărbătoare, vacanţă*
Work	*lucru*

Emergencies
Help!	*ajutor*
First aid	*primul ajutor*
Ambulance	*ambulanţa*
Clinic	*clinic*
Hospital	*spital*
Injured	*rănit*
Ill	*bolnav*
Pain	*durere*
Headache	*d. de cap*
Vomiting	*vărsătură*
Diarrhoea	*diaree*
Broken bone	*os rupt*

A bit of grammar

I am	*(eu)*	*sînt*
You are	*(tu)*	*eşti*
He, it; she is	*(el; ea)*	*eşte*
We are	*(noi)*	*sîntem*
You are	*(voi)*	*sînteţi*
They are	*(ei; ele)*	*sînt*

	(= possess)	*(with verb – eg, I have seen)*
I have	*am*	*am*
You have	*ai*	*ai*
He/she has	*are*	*a*
We have	*avem*	*am*
You have	*aveţi*	*aţi*
They have	*au*	*au*

Some regular verbs
Present tenses similarity to Latin is very clear.
a pleca = to arrive; *a merge* = to go
  a vedea = to see

plec	*merg*	*văd*
pleci	*mergi*	*vezi*
pleaca	*merge*	*vede*
plecam	*mergem*	*vedem*
plecaţi	*mergeţi*	*vedeţi*
plec	*merg*	*văd*

Note "phonetic" changes. These are normal.

a zice = to say; *a mulţumi* = thank
  a doborf = to get down (out of)

zic	*mulţunmesc*	*dobor*
zici	*mulţumeşti*	*dobori*
zice	*mulţume*	*doboară*
zicem	*mulţumim*	*doborîm*
ziceţi	*mulţumeţi*	*doborîţi*
zic	*mulţunesc*	*dobor*

a auzi = to hear, and similar verbs, have *aud* = I/they hear, *auzim* = we hear, *auziţi* = you hear. Note that *d* before *i* becomes *z*. Some verbs end *-ăsc*, *-ăşti*, etc instead of *-esc*, *-eşti*, etc. Verb infinitives' stress is on final syllables.

Nouns M. and n. nouns **without** definite articles (= the) have one form for sing. and one for plur. (f. have two). *-i* indicates plural for m. nouns and f. nouns ending in *-e*. *-e* indicates f. and n. plurs. Some nouns have a third (vocative) sing. form.

M. and n. nouns **with** definite articles have *-ul* and *-ului* in sing. unless the basic form ends in *-e*, when they have *-le* and *-elui*. Plurals are *-ii*, *-ilor*.

F. nouns change *-ă* to *-a* in sing., with gen./dat. *-ei*, unless the basic form ends *-eă*, when nom/acc. is *-eaua* (*Stea* = Star: the well-known football team is *Steaua* = The Star). Plurals are *-ele* or *-ile* and *-elor* or *-ilor*. *Steaua* is pronounced StAY-a-wa. The addition of def. arts. does not alter word stress.
N. nouns follow m. in sing., f. in plur.

TOP TRAVEL TITLES FROM SETTLE PRESS

The following books all feature in the highly popular WHERE TO GO IN series.

WHERE TO GO IN GREECE
by Trevor Webster
An up-to-date, easy-to-read, illustrated guide to
the islands and mainland centres.
"an exceptional title for both those seeking culture
and the sun". *The Bookseller*

£12.50 hard 0907070841 ☐
£7.99 paper 0907070876 ☐
New Edition
April 1991

WHERE TO GO IN AMERICA
by Ken Westcott Jones
A comprehensive guide to the attractions of each
part of America, interlaced with historical and
geographical detail. Many personal recommendations
from a well established writer.

£14.00 hard 0907070736 ☐
£7.99 paper 0907070744 ☐
Publication January 1991

WHERE TO GO IN SCOTLAND
by Bryn Frank
The myths, the magic and the taste (food and drink)
are all included in this clear guide to the Scottish
regions.

£12.50 hard 0907070884 ☐
£7.99 paper 0907070892 ☐
Publication June 1991

**CRETE AND THE CYCLADES
ISLANDS**
by Trevor Webster
The atmosphere of their stupendous mountains,
beaches, harbours and history is relayed by Trevor
Webster.

£9.99 hard 0907070388 ☐
£6.99 paper 0907070396 ☐
1987

WHERE TO GO IN SPAIN
A guide to the Iberian peninsula
by H. Dennis-Jones
Includes rating guides for all the Spanish coastal
regions and colourful descriptions of the interior.

£9.99 hard 0907070426 ☐
£5.99 paper 0907070434 ☐
1987

WHERE TO GO IN THE CANARY ISLANDS
by Reg Butler
Jetset nightlife, or peace-and-quiet; dramatic scenery
or city sightseeing and shopping – The Canary
Islands can help you choose which island can best fill
your requirements.

£14.00 hard 0907070671 ☐
£8.99 paper 090707068X ☐
1990

WHERE TO GO IN TUNISIA
by Reg Butler
While most visitors choose Tunisia for its year-round
Mediterranean sunshine, the book also describes the
fascination of Roman remains, Islamic cities, country
markets, oases and Berber strongholds.

£14.00 hard 0907070485 ☐
£8.99 paper 0907070493 ☐
1990

GREEK ISLAND DELIGHTS
by Trevor Webster
Trevor Webster explores 12 of the most popular and
magical isles in Greece, Crete, Corfu, Rhodes, Kos,
Samos, Skiathos, Mykonos, Santorini, Paros,
Thassos, Kephalonia and Zakynthos.

£14.00 hard 0907070604 ☐
£8.99 paper 0907070612 ☐

SETTLE PRESS (Reader Service Dept.), 10 Boyne Terrace Mews, London W11 3LR

Please send me the book(s) I have ticked. I am enclosing £
(prices cover postage and handling in UK).

Mr/Mrs/Miss . . . .

Address . . . .

. . . .

. . . .